Good Earth & Country Cooking

Good Earth & Country Cooking

BETTY GROFF and
JOSÉ WILSON

STACKPOLE BOOKS

GOOD EARTH & COUNTRY COOKING

Copyright © 1974 by Betty Groff and José Wilson
Published by
STACKPOLE BOOKS
Cameron and Kelker Streets
Harrisburg, Pa. 17105

Design by Helen Barrow

Library of Congress Cataloging in Publication Data

```
Groff, Betty.
    Good earth & country cooking.

    1.  Cookery, Mennonite.  2.  Cookery, American--
Pennsylvania.  I.  Wilson, José, joint author.
II.  Title.
TX715.G848              641.5'9748              73-23128
ISBN 0-8117-0737-7
```

PRINTED IN U.S.A.

ACKNOWLEDGMENTS

For their contributions to this book, I would like to thank the following people:

Ercol Acri, Arthur Kramer, Frank Errigo, Bill Fotiades, and Richard Hertzler, for capturing in their photographs the atmosphere and activities of Groff's Farm.

Saranna Miller and Bob Swain, for their beautiful sketches.

Kitty and John Brown, for allowing us to borrow from their collection of bygones for our illustrations.

My mother-in-law, Elizabeth Groff, for contributing some of her family recipes.

Erma Engle and Lena Fisher, for their untiring and devoted work behind the scenes, cooking and testing recipes.

Sharon Brown, Jean Sargen, and Betty Ward for their patience in transcribing and typing.

The Pfaltzgraff Company, for permission to use a food photograph taken at Groff's Farm.

Carolyn L. Charles, for historical background on the Mennonites of Lancaster County.

My good friend Jack, whose help was much appreciated.

Finally, very special thanks to the many wonderful people I have met through the restaurant, whose names I may not remember, but whose pleasure and praise I shall never forget. It was they who helped to make Groff's Farm a success and to spur me on to gather my recipes and remembrances in this book.

Betty Groff

ED. HAUN, DETROIT FREE PRESS

Here is my co-author, JOSÉ WILSON,
who put the story of Groff's Farm into words,
as I could never have done.
She's doing what comes naturally—
picking out vegetables in a farmer's market.

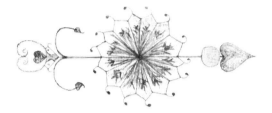

To my parents, who believed in me,
my husband, Abe, who backed me up all the way,
and my children, Charlie and Johnny,
who cheerfully tolerated a part-time mother.
Without their unfailing encouragement, support,
and help, Groff's Farm restaurant, and this book,
would never have been.

PHOTO CREDITS

DRAWINGS

CONTENTS

CONTENTS

CHAPTER I

I Cook Because I Love People

FROM the time I was a very little girl, I have loved people and loved food. To me they are inseparable. I grew up on a farm in Strasburg, Pennsylvania, where there were seldom fewer than twelve at table for every meal. The kitchen was the place that drew me, for it was always filled with laughter and activity and the smell of good things cooking.

My father's forebears, the Herrs, called Hern von Belried, came to Pennsylvania from the German part of Switzerland. Daddy, who is the family historian, says that there our ancestors were titled until 1593, but they gave up the title

Both my husband's family and mine are Mennonite,
and his father is a minister of the church.
These are my parents, above, *and his,* below.

and called themselves Herr—Mister. They were among the first settlers in Lancaster County; and the 1719 Hans Herr house, which is presently being restored, is the oldest standing house in the county.

Both my husband, Abram Groff, and I are descendants of Hans Herr, Mennonites, and tenth-generation natives. We say the Herrs knew what good was. They came to Lancaster County, stayed, and have never lived anywhere else. Often people are surprised that we don't speak in the Pennyslvania Dutch way, with slurred word endings and phrases backward, but in our part of the county we don't talk "Dutch," as they do around Manheim and Ephrata.

Visitors to our area often ask me who the Pennsylvania Dutch are, and how they came to live here. The Pennsylvania Dutch (Dutch is a corruption of *Deutsch*, or German) were Swiss-German Protestants who left the Palatinate in the early eighteenth century, seeking religious freedom, and settled in the eastern part of Pennsylvania, made up of the counties of Lancaster, York, Lebanon, and Berks. The Pennsylvania Dutch dialect some of the country folk speak is a mixture of old Palatinate German with some English words and phrases thrown in.

There are two kinds of Pennsylvania Dutch: Plain and Fancy. Fancy Dutch are members of the Lutheran and Reformed churches. Plain Dutch, chiefly Mennonites and Amish, are descendants of the Anabaptists, the left wing of the Reformation. They are stricter in their religious observances, dress simply, and worship at home, or in plain meeting houses, with ministers chosen by lot from the congregation.

The Pennsylvania Dutch were first and foremost farmers. In fact, we Lancaster County Mennonites are credited with having helped to lay the foundations of American agriculture by our care of the land and our innovative farming methods.

Like most hard-working farmers, we love to eat—and to eat heartily. We have a word, *feinschmecker,* which means a person who knows good food and eats plenty of it. Our cooking is half Old World and half New—a combination of the foods of our German ancestors, like ham and sausage, sauerkraut and noodles, and those that we adopted and grew here, such as corn, tomatoes, potatoes, squash, and pumpkins. You might say we took the best of both worlds.

In my family and Abe's, the father's side was strong on farming, the mother's on business, and that holds true to this day. My grandmother Herr, who ruled the family farm like a queen, was a very sharp business woman. She was my grandfather's second wife, and soon after they were married he lost one hand in an accident. Farmers need both hands if they are to be good providers, so Grandmother cleverly persuaded him that maybe his farmland wasn't all that productive and he should start a second business, butchering, to bring in extra income.

Grandmother was the first P.R. director a farmer ever had. When customers came to the butcher shop, she sat on the porch and talked to them. Soon it wasn't just a matter of coming to buy meat, but to hear what Amanda Herr had to say. She taught her two sons, Clarence and Emory, to think in a businesslike way, and by the time my father, Clarence, was fourteen years old, he was handling all the banking. In addition to raising cattle for butchering and keeping a dairy herd, the boys helped their mother dry sweet corn for sale and developed a special Persian melon seed, which became a big part of their trade. They sold melons in the summer, meat in the winter. To this day, my Dad is known for his melons, home-cured hams, dried beef, and bologna, although he is pretty well retired now.

In our community, it is the custom for the younger son,

when he marries, to be given the opportunity to buy the farm, although his parents retain a life right to it. When my father married, his father built a new house for him on the property; and Uncle Emory, the younger son, moved into the farmhouse with his bride, Aunt Ruth.

The whole family lived and worked as a unit. We'd talk about "up home" and "down home." Up home was our house, where we slept. Down home was the farm, where the action was.

When my Dad's older half sister, Aunt Suie, was widowed, she came to live at the farmhouse with her two children. Aunt Suie loved life and had a great sense of humor. Each of the women was a good cook and a specialist in her field. Aunt Ruth, who had worked for a baker, was the one who made pies. My mother had taken home economics and was great at yeast doughs and cakes. Aunt Suie was a whiz at peeling and paring, the fastest you ever saw; so she got to do all the vegetables.

When we got together at canning time to put up fruits and vegetables and relishes, it was like a big family party, never a drag. I can remember peeling 9 sacks of apples in one day, to make 100 quarts of applesauce. To this day, I get a kick out of freezing corn and making relishes and apple butter with my family and friends. There is something creative and rewarding about it. When people ask me how I learned to be such a good cook, I tell them that with so many good cooks in the family, if you didn't do something well, you never got asked again. That puts you on your mettle.

By the time I was thirteen I was entering canning and baking contests. My lemon chiffon cakes won in both the adult and school division and I came home with a nice pocketful of money. The only real disaster I had was with a tuna-noodle casserole I learned to make in home economics class at high

Mince Pie Without Meat

Take 1 cup molasses 1 cup sugar 1 cup vinegar
1 cup flour 3 cups of water 3 eggs
1 teaspoonful of soda 1 teaspoonful cinnamon
1 teaspoonful cloves

A friend loaned my mother two handwritten cookbooks dating back to the nineteenth century. You can see from these recipes how little our cooking has changed. One of the women even has the same name as mine, Elizabeth Groff.

Soft Ginger Bread

Stir to a cream 1 cup of butter, and ½ cup brown sugar. Add to this 2 cup of cooking molasses, 1 cup sweet milk 1 tablespoon ginger 1 teaspoon cinnamon beat all together thoroughly.

Then add 3 eggs beat the white separatly. beat into this 2 cups of flour 1 teaspoon soda dissolve the soda in a spoonful of water and last add 2 more cups flour butter & paper two long bread pans divide the mixture bake in a moderate oven. This cake requires long and slow baking. 30 or 40 min. Sweet or Sour milk will do. I prefer sour the cake is much lighter

Ida Groff

Lemon Pie

1 cup sugar 2 table spoon cornstarch 1 cup boiling water butter half the size of an egg the grated rind and juice of one lemon cook together till clear.

When cold add the yoke of an egg. line the plate with the paste and bake then fill. putting on the white of an egg with a little sugar for icing then put in the oven and brown.

Lizzie Groff

Spung Cake

12 egg 10 oz of sifted flour dried near the fire
1 lb of loaf sugar powdered and sifted   12 drops
essence of lemon a grated nut meg 1 teaspoonfull
powdered sinnamon and mace mixed beat the
eggs as light as possible eggs for the spung or
almond cakes require more beating than for any
other purpose beat the sugar by degrees into the
eggs beat very hard and continue to beat
some time after the sugar is all in   no sort of
sugar but loaf will make light spung cake
stir in gradually the spice and essence of the lemon
then by degrees put in the flour a little at a
time stirring round the mixture very slowly
with a knife if the flour is stirred in too hard
the cake will be tough it must be done lightly
and gently so that the top of the mixture will
be covered with bubbles as soon as the flour is all
in begin to bake it as setting will injure it
put it in small tins well buttered or in one
large tin pan the thinner the better for the
spung cake fill the small tins about half full
grate loaf sugar over the tops of each before
you set them in the oven spung requires a
very quick oven peticarlarly at the bottom
it should be baked as fast as possible or it will be
tough and heavy however light it may have been
before it went into the oven it is of all cakes
most liable to be spoiled in baking when taken
out of the tins the cakes should be spread in a
sive to cool if baked in large cake it should be
iced a large cake of twelve eggs should be baked
at least 1 hour in a quick oven for small cakes
10 minutes is gennerly suffissient if they get
very much out of shape in baking it is a sign
that the oven is too slow

Curren Shrub

For 3 quarts of shrub take 3 pints of curren juice
4 lbs of sugar boil it a few moments and then
let it cool and then add 1 quart of brandy

school. I was so proud of myself that I asked Mother if I could make it for supper that night. Daddy took one taste and said to me, "Child, you know I love good meat and good vegetables. The very worst thing you can do is mess everything up together and ruin it all. If you'll excuse me, I'm going down to the farm where they're having beefsteak and gravy and new potatoes." With that, he gave me a kiss and left.

I never made it again until three or four years ago. My son Charlie came back from camp raving about the tuna-noodle casserole they'd had. I made it just for the two of us, knowing Abe wouldn't eat it. Charlie took two or three bites and put his fork down. I said to him, "You asked for it. Why aren't you eating it?" His answer really floored me. "Well, Mom, I'd rather have it cold, like we had it in camp." From there on, tuna-noodle casserole was off my list.

If the women in our family were good cooks, they had to be. The men had excellent palates and a kind of sixth sense about food. My Uncle Emory's nose was so acute that when he came up from the butcher shop, before he even set foot on the porch, he could tell whether the peas were salted enough, or whether something had been forgotten in whatever dish was being cooked. Our foods are so simple that if you cultivate your sense of smell, you can't miss; you don't even have to taste. Now I find that I can walk through the kitchen and tell just by sniffing if things are properly seasoned.

My brother Ray inherited that same sense of smell, and he is a pretty good cook himself. It is customary in our community for all the aunts and uncles to have the new bride and groom to dinner. After they have been entertained, the newly-weds have to have all those relatives back at one go—sometimes as many as thirty to forty people. This is probably the most important dinner you ever give, because your relatives are highly critical and it is a point of honor to do the very best you can. Ray and his wife, Lete, were giving their first family dinner, and she got sick. Ray went into the kitchen and finished off the turkey, made bread filling, and prepared all the vegetables. By the time Lete came downstairs everything was just about ready. The dinner went off beautifully, and Daddy was really proud of Ray.

I guess I get my love of people and my gregariousness from my grandmother and my father. Uncle Emory was the nature lover, the fisherman, and a minister of our church. Daddy was the businessman. He did all the selling and loved every minute of it. I was active in 4H and all the Mennonite church and social activities, and in high school I joined the band. Mother wanted me to play the harp, a nice ladylike instrument, but all his life Daddy had yearned to play the horn. The teacher said, after one lesson, that I was a born horn player. As I was only thirteen, and small for my age, the man in the music store advised Daddy to buy me a cornet, rather than a trumpet. I started as second cornet and in a year I was playing first chair, the only girl among all those boys. I think our guests are often surprised to see me get out my cornet after dinner and start playing, but it is something I really love doing. In every way, I'm my father's daughter.

When Abe and I were married in 1955, we knew farming was the life for us. That had been his background, and mine. We looked at several farms, none of which were quite what Abe wanted. Finally Daddy discovered this place in Mount Joy. The farmland was beautiful and the farm buildings were great; but the stone farmhouse, which was built in 1756, was in really bad shape—the roof sagging and the old hand-cut fieldstone smeared with mortar. Abe was so impressed with the land, he hardly looked at the house. All I remember thinking about was the size of the rooms and how pretty those deep-set windows were.

Daddy, who knows a lot about real estate, said we shouldn't be put off by appearances. The house had been neglected, but it was a diamond in the rough. If we decided we wanted it, he would fix up the house for us. All that winter Abe and Daddy and some Amish friends worked on it, sandblasting the fieldstone and putting in recessed mortar, restoring the old random-width floor boards. By the time we moved in the following year, after the Fourth of July, it was one of the most beautiful old houses I had ever seen.

We Mennonites have another custom that I think is nice. The wife provides the furniture for the home, the man the animals and equipment for the farm. Everything else they buy together. I set about buying antiques and Abe learned a lot about them by refinishing the old furniture, which really started him on his hobby of making reproduction furniture. He also learned about meat by helping Daddy in the butcher shop that first winter when we lived at my home, before we moved onto our farm. He got a feel for the good cuts and picked up the tricks and techniques of carving and seasoning meat. I always say I may be the butcher's daughter, but he sure acts like the butcher's son. He knows meats much better than I do.

Abe's food background and mine are complementary in many ways. Because of the butcher shop, our family was strong on meats. Abe's father was in the chicken and dairy business, and there were nine children in the household; so the Groffs used more eggs, milk, and chicken, and had lots of pies and cakes. There it was pie for breakfast, dinner, and supper. His mother was an excellent manager, and fed all those children well on a limited budget. She can whip up meals without recipes and she is great on baked vegetable dishes, like her salsify casserole.

Abe loves his pie and cake. He's the one I try my recipes out on. If he likes a pie, that's good enough for me.

About four or five years after we started farming, I began to get a little bit restless. My life at home had been so active and full that I had always thought of a farm as a place like my father's with lots of people coming and going and telling you everything that was going on. I really missed that.

I had worked in offices before I was married, so at first I thought I might take a part-time job in a bank. My father wouldn't hear of it. With the farm and the house and our first son to look after, he felt I should stay home and work at my marriage. So I had to come up with another idea. My first thought was to make candy, but that is really hard work for very little return. I could slave making 100 pounds of hand-dipped candy and sell it all in three weeks.

Then one day Mother told me, as a joke, that a local restaurant called The Willows was looking for a Mennonite girl to cook dinners in her own home for special bus groups— camera clubs, librarians, teachers, and so on. Maybe thirty-five to forty people at a time. "Why, Betty, that would be a great idea for you," she said. "Your dining room would hold forty people, wouldn't it?"

I took her seriously. I thought that sounded terrific. Mother and Daddy didn't believe I could do it, until I reminded them that just a little while before I'd had my family dinner party for thirty-two uncles and aunts and cousins, and it had been a smashing success. If I could cook for thirty-two supercritical people who knew what they were eating, the world's toughest audience, why couldn't I cook for people who had never tasted our kind of food before? Mother and Daddy were still dubious. They just couldn't see why people would drive twenty-two miles into the Pennsylvania Dutch country to eat one of our meals.

I talked it over with Abe and he didn't mind one little bit, as long as it didn't interfere with the farming schedule. So that's how I started. First of all, it was groups, but then

*Ours is a working farm and one of the crops we raise
is feed corn. Our elder son, Charlie, is driving the tractor.
The younger one, Johnny, is with my husband, Abe,
and our Labrador, Blackie.*

little by little the local people started coming, and that's what
pleased me most. I had taken a shoofly pie to my orthodontist
and he asked if I would do a party for a group of twelve. The
guests told others in their churches or clubs, and gradually
the local business started to build.

My big break came when Mrs. John Hartman, a lady in
Strasburg who knew my family, brought Craig Claiborne,

the Food Editor of the *New York Times*, to dinner. I didn't know who he was until afterward, and if I had I'd have been scared silly. Once his story came out in the paper, business really boomed. Up until then, we had never taken groups of less than twelve, but Craig said that for his readership we would have to take smaller reservations, and that is the way we do it now. We have tables of different sizes; we don't serve family style at one big table where you sit with just anyone. The maximum we can take is eighty people for each sitting, because we want to keep that feeling of being in a home. One recent and satisfying experience was watching the delight of a group of visiting electronics engineers from the People's Republic of China thoroughly enjoying our food.

Up until the story appeared in the *Times*, Daddy had been very cautious about telling anyone about my business. He felt I had to succeed on my own merits, and I'm glad he did.

At first Abe wasn't involved in the restaurant, but by the time the first newspaper story came out, he was doing all the carving. He still got up at 4:30 A.M. and farmed all day, and it didn't seem fair that he should be working in the background and getting none of the credit. So when the *Washington Evening Star* came here to do a story, I saw to it that they photographed Abe carving. When the story was printed, there he was heading off the woman's page in full color, while I was on the second page in black and white.

That was the best thing that could have happened. The people who came asked to meet him, and their enjoyment of him made him see how much more fun it was to be up front in the dining room instead of back in the kitchen. He started to put more emphasis on the restaurant and less on farming. Now we have sold our dairy herd and he no longer has to get up at 4:30 and milk the cows. You've no idea what a change that has made in our lives.

Abe learned about meat from my father;
so he has always done the ordering, cooking, and
carving of the hams and prime rib roasts we serve.

One thing just naturally seems to lead to another. In the fall of 1969, José Wilson, who was writing a book for the Time-Life Foods of the World series on American regional cooking, came to interview me about Pennsylvania Dutch food. She wrote about us, Time-Life photographed here, and the editors asked me to contribute some of my recipes and work with John Clancy, their test kitchen chef.

Oddly enough, José had known my Dad for some time, ever since she'd done an article on the Pennsylvania Dutch country for *House & Garden,* of which she was then Food and Features Editor. He had never said a word to her about me and my enterprise. She heard about me through Jim Beard and Mrs. Hartman.

When the Time-Life book, *American Cooking: The Eastern Heartland,* came out in 1971, I sold a lot of copies in the restaurant because it had some of my recipes and pictures of me and my family.

Everyone asked me when I was going to do my own cookbook. I'm no writer, but I knew I could do it with José's help. To me, she had written more understandingly about us and our food than anyone else I could think of. Although she is English, we have the same kind of background. She grew up in the farm country of Cumberland where the food was very much like ours, simple and satisfying, with home-cured hams and fresh pork sausage, home-grown vegetables and fruits. Her mother made piecrust with butter and lard, as we do.

Our kind of food is the kind she is, as she says, "eternally hungry for." So it was natural for us to team up and write this book. I hope it will bring many more people to Groff's Farm. I need people in order to be happy. I need to cook for them, to talk with them, and to make them happy in turn.

Abe and I like to get dressed up in the evening and welcome our guests at the front door.

CHAPTER II

For Every Food There Is A Season

GROWING UP IN THE COUNTRY and on a farm, as I did, my love of food grew with me. All our family loved to eat; it was one of our greatest pleasures, and we never compromised on quality. As Daddy always said, "The best isn't too good for us."

We raised most of our own food, and so we lived and ate according to the seasons. In fall and winter, after the butchering, we would have plenty of fresh meat. During the rest of the year there would be home-canned beefsteak and pork loin, home-cured hams, dried beef and bologna, fried sausage and spareribs, put down in crocks and sealed with lard. Down cellar the shelves were filled with quarts of applesauce and apple butter, mincemeat and relishes. You never saw such a beautiful sight.

I think one of the delights of the past that we miss today is the excitement of eating foods in season, when they are at their best and freshest. At home on the farm we looked forward to spring, which brought the early asparagus and rhubarb, the first garden cutting lettuce and tender spinach, and the delicate, immature dandelion greens we ate with a hot bacon dressing.

Gradually, the earth yielded more good things—spring onions and radishes, sugar peas, baby carrots and potatoes. In summer there was a wealth of vegetables and fruits to eat and to can or pickle—garden peas and green beans, corn and tomatoes, eggplant, peppers and squash, ripe red strawberries and cherries, and the sweet little berries that grew wild—wineberries, black raspberries, huckleberries, and blackberries. Fall brought sweet potatoes, pole lima beans, melons, pumpkins, and apples.

Certain food combinations were traditional with us; the flavors just naturally seemed to go together. Ham with asparagus or with green beans, cole slaw, and scraped potatoes. Shad with baby new potatoes and sweet little peas. Fried chicken with corn fritters and chow chow. Pork pot roast with turnips and potatoes, mashed together with the pork broth, buttered spinach, and apple pie. Sausage with fried potatoes and raw sliced onion. Fried ham slices with warm rice pudding and canned sour cherries.

I'm speaking now of our part of Pennsylvania, Lancaster County. Abe and I are tenth-generation natives, and we have never known anything but our own food. There are just as many Pennsylvania Dutch in Berks County, but in many ways our cooking is worlds apart. We cook simply, but we have all kinds of little tricks to bring out the natural flavor and goodness of food—things that are second nature to me, but that I find come as a surprise to my guests. For instance, we boil our vegetables in very little water, seasoned with both sugar and salt, then pour browned butter over them; and we brown the flour used to thicken gravies, soups, and certain sauces. Saffron goes in with chicken, to give the stock a very subtle and delicate taste, and a grating of nutmeg spices berry pies and lemonade.

While we are on the subject of Pennsylvania Dutch cooking, I'd like to clear up that misconception about the "seven sweets and seven sours" we are supposed to serve at every meal. We do like our sweets (which include pies, cakes and puddings, preserves and home-canned fruits) and our sours, or relishes, but we pick only those that go with the type of meat we are eating. Naturally, the more meats served at one meal, the more sweets and sours. While for company dinners we would provide plenty of each, so every guest could find something to suit his or her palate, for family dinners and everyday eating we would have maybe one or two relishes and a couple of desserts. With beef we might have a hot and spicy mustard pickle; with ham a sweet and spicy watermelon rind or cantaloupe.

So if you would like to duplicate a real Lancaster County meal at home, pick any of the menus in this chapter. You will be eating the way we do—and, I hope, enjoying it as much as we do.

Note: All recipes serve six unless otherwise noted.

A few of our Pennsylvania Dutch foods:
ham and bean soup, Montgomery pie, and homemade relishes.

A spring still life at the edge of the trout pond.

TWO SPRING LUNCHEONS

STEWED CRACKERS
SLICED COLD SMOKED TONGUE *or* COLD SMOKED MEATS
DANDELION SALAD WITH HOT BACON DRESSING

This is a very simple meal, the kind we would have on the farm in the early spring, when the young dandelion greens appeared in the meadows. You have to pick them very, very young, before the flowers bloom, or they'll be bitter. It really doesn't take long to pick enough for 6 people, about 1 cup per serving. Take a small sharp knife and get right down under the ground so you cut off the little bunch of leaves with about half an inch of the root. Put them in the sink, strip down that brown edge and nip the leaves off at the root, so they all fall apart—and there's your salad. They are best when picked in late March or April, but in shady areas you can get them later, up into early June. If you have a lawn full of dandelions, this is a way to get rid of them before they flower and spread their seeds—and you'll have some very good eating into the bargain.

Stewed crackers are something we always used to eat to soothe an upset stomach, or the older people would have them as a Sunday dish; but actually they are nice and light for luncheon: bland, but a pleasant contrast to the smoky flavor of the tongue—or any other smoked meats like beef, ham, or bologna. There's one little trick in it and that is the browned butter. Browned butter is a must in our cookery and something that intrigues folks outside the Pennsylvania Dutch area.

33

It gives such a delicious flavor, like a rather spicy caramel, and it does great things for anything plain, especially vegetables. We always use browned butter on our vegetables, and it has brought more comments than anything else. You can brown butter ahead and leave it for days in the refrigerator, then just warm it up a bit, stirring it, and pour it over whatever you are serving.

STEWED CRACKERS

  6 cups (3 packages) saltine crackers
     Freshly ground black pepper to taste
½ cup boiling water
  6 tablespoons Browned Butter (see method below)
  1 cup half-and-half (or half milk, half cream)

Arrange the crackers in layers in a casserole with a cover. Sprinkle with pepper. Pour the boiling water over the crackers and immediately put on the cover, leaving them to swell up.

Make or melt the Browned Butter in a 1-quart saucepan and stir in the half-and-half. Heat until very hot, but not boiling; then remove cover from casserole and pour the hot liquid over the crackers. Replace the cover and let them steam another 5 minutes, until very soft on the bottom and rather chewy on top.

TO MAKE BROWNED BUTTER

Melt ½ pound butter over medium-low heat in a heavy 1-quart saucepan (the butter has a tendency to boil over, so make sure you have a big enough pan). After it melts, stir occasionally until it starts to brown. Remove from heat before it burns. If it gets too dark, it will lose its flavor and become bitter; it should be just a rich nut brown.

DANDELION SALAD WITH
HOT BACON DRESSING

    6 cups loosely packed young dandelion greens, washed and
        cleaned
 ½ pound bacon
    6 eggs
    2 tablespoons cornstarch
1½ teaspoons salt
    3 tablespoons granulated sugar
 ⅓ cup cider vinegar
    2 cups milk

Tear the washed greens as you would for any garden salad
and place in a bowl. Fry the bacon until crisp; remove and
drain on paper towels, saving the fat for the dressing. Boil 4
of the eggs for 15 minutes; then cool under running water so
they will be ready to peel by the time the dressing is finished.
Crumble the bacon, or break into bits. Mix together the dry
ingredients, then the remaining two eggs, slightly beaten, and
the vinegar. Blend well. Stir in the milk and 4 tablespoons of
the hot bacon fat. Bring to a boil, stirring constantly with a
wooden spoon or wire whip, and boil 1 minute. Mix in half
the bacon bits. Cool slightly. Pour some of the hot dressing
over the dandelion greens and toss lightly. Garnish with the
hard-boiled eggs, shelled and sliced, and remaining bacon
bits, and serve immediately. Have remaining dressing in a side
dish, to be added as desired.

FRIED BROOK TROUT   SUGAR PEAS   HOMEMADE NOODLES
SPRING ONIONS AND RADISHES WITH BUTTERED BREAD
SPANISH CREAM

We Pennsylvania Dutch are fish lovers as well as meat eaters. In the spring, the boys would go out to fish for suckers and bluegills; and the fish man who came around every week would bring us shad, clams, and oysters. Abe and I stocked a trout pond out front, down by the springhouse, and we can have fresh trout any old time we feel like it.

A lot of people don't like to cook trout with the head on, and I don't like to do them any other way. If you leave the head on, it is so easy to fillet after it has been broiled or fried; you just put the fork under the top of the spine and bring the head back toward the tail and the whole fillet comes right off.

Sugar peas, which are edible-pod peas, like the Chinese snow peas or the French *mange-tout*, have always been part of our cooking. You can go as far back as any of the written-down recipes and find sugar peas. For years no one but Lancaster County people ate the pod. My grandmother Herr grew the more common type of sugar pea with a broad flat pod. After I was married I bought sugar pea seed and planted it. When Mother came to help harvest the peas, she thought I must have got the wrong thing because they were quite different; they looked more like a green bean, with a much rounder pod. Then she remembered that this was another variety her mother used to grow when she was a little girl, a kind called the sickle pod sugar pea. Someone must have saved the seed all through the years and sold it to the seed people to grow commercially (we Pennsylvania Dutch are great at saving and passing down seeds; we are a very thrifty folk). When we cooked the peas we found they were much sweeter and tenderer, the most delicious I'd ever eaten. I saved the seed from year to year; then they got a blight and we lost them, so now we are back to the flat pod pea. We usually serve them the first three and a half weeks they are in season, from Memorial Day on, and people who aren't from our part of the country just rave about them.

Vegetables are so wonderful in season, freshly picked. We pull the spring onions and radishes and eat them as a salad with buttered bread, leaving the lovely leafy green tops on the onions; it's such a colorful combination.

Homemade noodles—that's another big thing with us. When I was little, I wanted to make some extra spending money so mother said why didn't I make noodles and sell them, anyone could do that. I'd roll them out on a big board, as thin as I could get them, hang them out on the washline to dry a little, then roll them up like a jellyroll and slice them thick or thin. I liked the wide ones, but Daddy preferred his narrow. I love to make noodles and though mother used only the egg yolks, I find they are easier to roll if you put the whole egg in—easier still, of course, if you have one of those Italian pasta machines.

Most of our cookbooks are handed down from family to family, and you'll always find recipes for Spanish cream; everybody loves it. The secret is not cooking it too long. When the custard just starts to coat the spoon, pour it into the mold. You'd think it wasn't going to do anything, but as it sets it separates and becomes clear on the top and creamy on the bottom.

FRIED BROOK TROUT

For each serving allow 1 trout or half a trout, according to size. Clean the whole trout, removing the eyes, but leave the head and fins on. Shake trout in a paper or plastic bag with ½ cup flour, ½ teaspoon salt, and a dash of pepper for each trout. Remove. Lightly salt inside of fish.

For each trout, melt 3 tablespoons butter in a heavy skillet and fry until golden brown on both sides. Serve with a lemon twist on top and pop a sprig of parsley in the eye socket.

To fillet, gently lift the head and place a fork behind the gill and center backbone. Pull the head back toward the tail and the whole backbone will come away from the fish, leaving the bottom fillet on the platter. Flip the fish over and lift out the spine with all the bones intact.

SUGAR PEAS

1 quart fresh sugar peas
½ cup water
¾ teaspoon salt
½ teaspoon sugar

With sugar peas, as with any fresh vegetable, it is very important not to overboil. You need very little water in the pan to cook a vegetable quickly. For almost any of the tiny and medium-sized vegetables—sugar peas, peas, beans, limas, corn —a few minutes in boiling water and steam is plenty, and we feel every vegetable benefits from being cooked with sugar as well as salt.

Wash the sugar peas and put the whole pods in a saucepan with the water, salt, and sugar. Cover and bring to a boil. When the water comes to a full boil, remove the pan from the heat and let the vegetables stand until you are ready to serve them—not more than 5 minutes, if possible. The color will change from bright to dull green and they will become limp. They should be served rather crisp to the bite. Drain and serve, with or without Browned Butter (see p. 34).

HOMEMADE NOODLES

2 to 2½ cups flour
½ teaspoon salt
3 whole eggs
1 tablespoon cold water

Put 2 cups flour and the salt on a pastry board or in a deep mixing bowl. Make a well in the middle of the flour and add the eggs and the water. Gradually mix the dry ingredients into the liquid ones with your hand or a heavy wooden spoon until well blended. Gather into a ball and knead until very smooth on a floured board, adding a little more of the remaining flour if the dough sticks to your hands, but only enough to make a firm dough. Knead for approximately 10 minutes; then cover with plastic wrap until ready to roll out. Cut dough into thirds and roll out one third at a time.

Dust a little flour over and under the dough and roll it to a paper thin rectangle. Trim the edges and flour both sides generously. Starting at one end of the dough, roll up into a neat, tight roll, jelly-roll fashion. Take a very sharp cook's knife or butcher knife and cut the roll into thin slices, ¼ inch wide. As the slices fall onto the board, toss them lightly with your hand so they do not stick together. Unroll the noodles and let them dry on paper towels before cooking.

To cook, bring 4 quarts salted water to a rapid boil in a large pot. Add 1 tablespoon oil to prevent the noodles sticking together, drop them in, and cook at a rapid boil until just tender to the bite. Drain and serve with the trout.

NOTE

The noodles can be covered tightly with plastic wrap and refrigerated for a couple of days. If stored in the freezer, they will keep several months.

SPANISH CREAM

2 tablespoons unflavored gelatin
3 cups milk
½ cup sugar
¼ teaspoon salt
3 eggs, separated
1 teaspoon vanilla

Soak the gelatin in the milk until dissolved. Scald the milk in the top of a double boiler and mix in the sugar and salt. Pour the hot mixture slowly over the egg yolks, which have been lightly beaten. Return to the top of the double boiler and cook over hot water until slightly thickened, about 4 minutes, stirring constantly. Remove from the heat and fold in the stiffly beaten egg whites and the vanilla. Dip a mold into cold water, then pour the cream mixture into it. Chill until set; then unmold and serve with whipped cream.

Note: If you make this in individual molds, use less gelatin.

FOUR SPRING DINNERS

BAKED SHAD AND FRIED SHAD ROE
POTATOES BOILED IN THEIR JACKETS   GARDEN PEAS
GARDEN CUTTING LETTUCE WITH SWEET AND SOUR DRESSING
RHUBARB CRUMBLE

Shad is one fish that has always been very popular in the Pennsylvania Dutch country. I can remember how my grandfather looked forward to it in the spring—and to the fried shad roe, which in our house was traditionally reserved for the menfolk. By the end of the shad season, the little new garden peas would be in, and these, with plain boiled potatoes, just seemed to be the best of all vegetables to have with the rich, oily fish. The first garden lettuce we'd have would be the cutting lettuce—a pale, delicate, looseleaf lettuce. Lots of times the family would plant it with their tobacco beds, where the ground was sterilized, cover it with muslin, and water it daily so the seeds grew quickly. If you didn't have tobacco beds, you'd have one little square of about three feet in your garden, with a burlap bag over it to keep it moist. The dressing is very Pennsylvania Dutch, very typical. We like our sweet-and-sours really sweet, but if you don't, you can cut down on the sugar.

In spring, we had rhubarb, too. My husband loved it in any shape or form, though it left me cold. I was always looking for different ways to do it. The rhubarb crumble is something I used to make and forgot all about until one evening I was going to serve rhubarb at one of the Colonial night dinners. I hunted through all my cookbooks and found it in a Canadian co-op cookbook sent to me by a friend in Saskatchewan, and it was just about identical with the one I used to make. Well, after the dinner I was talking to this Canadian couple and the man said, "We had the best time tonight, that rhubarb was so good, just the way my grandmother made it," and where do you think they were from? Saskatchewan. I guess it proves that our style of cooking is pretty universal.

BAKED SHAD

Clean and split a 3-pound shad. Put skin side down in a buttered shallow baking dish, sprinkle with salt and pepper, and cover with slices of bacon. Bake in a 400° oven for 30 minutes.

FRIED SHAD ROE

    3 pairs shad roe
    ¼ cup flour
    ½ teaspoon salt
      Dash of pepper
    4 tablespoons bacon drippings or butter

Shake the roe in a paper bag with the flour and seasonings until coated. Melt the bacon drippings or butter in a skillet and fry the roe until golden brown on both sides, about 5 to 6 minutes a side.

POTATOES BOILED IN THEIR JACKETS

Scrub 6 medium white potatoes and boil, whole and unpeeled, in salted water until tender, about 25 minutes. Serve with plenty of butter, salt and pepper, to mash into the potatoes when they are cut.

GARDEN PEAS

1½ pounds shelled green peas
 1 teaspoon salt
 1 teaspoon sugar
 1 tablespoon butter
 ½ cup water

Bring the peas to a boil in the water, salt, sugar, and butter. Boil 2 minutes only, then remove from the heat and drain. If you like, pour Browned Butter (see p. 34) over them.

SWEET AND SOUR DRESSING

 ½ cup cider vinegar
 1 cup sugar
   Salt, freshly ground black pepper
 ¼ teaspoon celery salt or celery seed
 1 cup evaporated milk

Blend together the vinegar, sugar, salt and pepper to taste, celery salt or seed, and evaporated milk. Pour over the cutting lettuce and toss lightly.

RHUBARB CRUMBLE

 3 cups diced rhubarb
 ¾ cup granulated sugar
 ¼ cup water
 1 cup brown sugar
1¼ cups flour
 ½ cup butter

Mix the rhubarb, granulated sugar, and water and put in a baking dish. Mix the brown sugar, flour, and butter quickly with your fingers or a pastry blender until crumbly. Spread on top of the rhubarb and bake in a 350° oven for 40 minutes. Serve warm or cold, with or without heavy or whipped cream.

FRIED HAM SLICES   ASPARAGUS GROFF
MASHED POTATOES   RHUBARB SAUCE

There aren't many spring meats on a farm, so we would take a center cut out of one of our home-cured hams, slice and fry it, and eat it with the early asparagus, the first of the garden vegetables. We always had asparagus with the fried ham; they just naturally go together in our cooking. You had to go out first thing in the morning and cut the asparagus off right at the ground, and I remember this was one of the few jobs I really hated as a child. Sometimes, instead of a dessert, we'd have a side dish of rhubarb with our meat; the tartness went well with it.

FRIED HAM SLICES

Take 2 1-pound slices of center-cut home-cured ham, 1 inch thick, and fry in 2 tablespoons shortening in a heavy skillet until golden brown on both sides. If you want gravy with your ham and mashed potatoes, remove the ham, add 1 cup water to the skillet, cover, and simmer 10 minutes. Thicken with 1 tablespoon cornstarch mixed to a paste with 2 tablespoons water.

ASPARAGUS GROFF

  2 pounds asparagus
⅔ cup water
  1 teaspoon salt
  1 teaspoon sugar
  1 cup medium white sauce
  4 tablespoons Browned Butter (see p. 34)
  4 slices toast, cut in squares and buttered

44

Wash and trim the asparagus. Usually there is at least an inch of waste at the bottom of each stalk, which should be snapped off. Cut the spears into 1-inch pieces and put in a saucepan with the water, salt, and sugar. Cover and boil until just tender; five minutes should be adequate. If the asparagus is not tender by then, remove the pan from the heat and let the asparagus stand until tender.

Transfer the asparagus to a serving dish with a slotted spoon; pour the white sauce over it and the browned butter over the top. Garnish with a few toast squares and serve the rest of the toast separately. Serve at once.

MASHED POTATOES

Peel, boil, and mash 6 large potatoes in the usual way. I like to whip in a small amount (about 1/2 cup) evaporated milk to keep the potatoes rich and fluffy, and always lots of butter, with salt and pepper to taste. Leftover mashed potatoes can be made into Potato Cakes (see p. 125), or used for Potato Filling (see p. 94).

RHUBARB SAUCE

   1/2 cup water
   3 cups diced pink rhubarb
   1 cup granulated sugar
   1/2 cup brown sugar
   1/4 teaspoon salt
   3 tablespoons cornstarch dissolved in 1/4 cup water
   1 tablespoon lemon juice

Bring the water to a boil and add the rhubarb. Boil 3 minutes; next, add the granulated and brown sugar and the salt. Then stir in the dissolved cornstarch and the lemon juice. Cook until slightly thick.

BREADED PORK LOIN   SCRAPED NEW POTATOES
SCRAPED WHOLE BABY CARROTS
SPINACH AND MUSHROOMS VINAIGRETTE
STRAWBERRY SHORTCAKE

When we lived on the farm and had the butcher shop, Mother always canned pork loin and beefsteak during the winter, to eat in spring. The pork loin made a great quick meal; we took it from the jar, dipped it in egg, rolled it in bread crumbs, and fried it until it was golden brown. With a vegetable, potatoes, and fruit you had a meal fit for a king in 15 minutes. The jellied broth from the jar went into a saucepan to make the most delicious gravy. Nowadays I use fresh pork loin, but I still like to pan-fry it the same way.

There are all kinds of ways of doing potatoes, but when the first new potatoes are dug, scraped potatoes are by far the best. Scraping gives potatoes a flavor they just don't have when you pare them with a knife; people ask me if there is sugar in them.

When I lived at home, I hated scraping potatoes with a passion. I declared that if I ever got married I'd never scrape a potato again, but after I started cooking for the family, and especially since the dinner guests enjoy them so, I probably scrape more potatoes now than I ever did before. When your heart is in your work and you know you are giving others pleasure, it's amazing how your attitude changes. I remember one night I told everyone in the dining room at one of our Colonial dinners that one of the surprises would be scraped new potatoes. Later on, I heard this little fellow from North Carolina saying to his mother, "Do y'all know what ah liked best—ah liked those new-bawhn potatoes"; so now I always think of them as new-born potatoes.

We make our shortcake in one big pan, farm-style. When you are cooking for a dozen or more people, you can't do it individually, but it tastes just as good.

The salad of spinach and mushrooms is certainly not traditional, although we always raised spinach, but it is one of my own favorites with this menu.

BREADED PORK LOIN

3 pounds pork loin, cut in slices ½ inch thick
2 beaten eggs
1 teaspoon salt
¼ teaspoon freshly ground pepper
1 cup dry bread crumbs
Butter for pan-frying

Dip the loin slices in the egg, season with salt and pepper, and then dip in the crumbs. Pan-fry in the butter in a heavy skillet over medium heat until golden brown on both sides—not more than 15 minutes a side or the loin will become very dry.

SCRAPED NEW POTATOES

When you buy new potatoes, check by scraping at one spot with your thumbnail to see if the skins are loose enough to scrape easily with a paring knife. Scrape as many as you think your guests can eat (you can do them ahead and leave them in cold water); then cook in boiling salted water until just tender. Drain and serve with browned butter. The potato usually bursts open a little bit, which is perfect for absorbing the butter. Leftover potatoes can be browned whole and served with fried ham.

SCRAPED WHOLE BABY CARROTS

Scrape these like the potatoes and boil in salted water until tender. Serve with Browned Butter (see p. 34).

SPINACH AND MUSHROOMS VINAIGRETTE

     1 pound spinach, stemmed and pinched in pieces
    ¼ pound mushrooms, sliced
    ¾ cup olive oil
     2 tablespoons red wine
     2 tablespoons vinegar
    ¼ teaspoon salt
    ½ teaspoon onion salt
       Freshly ground pepper to taste

Put spinach and mushrooms in a bowl. Combine the dressing ingredients in a jar and shake well to combine. Pour as much dressing as needed over the salad and toss well.

STRAWBERRY SHORTCAKE

     4 eggs
    ½ cup (scant) lard
     2 cups (scant) sugar
     5 cups flour
     4 teaspoons baking powder
    ½ teaspoon salt
    1¾ cups milk
     4 cups sliced, sugared strawberries
       Whole strawberries for the topping
    ½ pint heavy cream, whipped

Beat the eggs. Beat with the lard and sugar until fluffy. Sift together the flour, baking powder, and salt. Add to the egg mixture alternately with the milk until the batter is smooth.

Pour into a 9 x 13-inch baking pan and bake in a 350° oven for 50 minutes. To serve, cut in 3 x 4-inch slices and split. Put the sugared, sliced strawberries between the layers, with lightly whipped cream and whole berries on top. Or you can put the shortcake in a soup bowl and pour sweetened milk over it.

HAM AND GREEN BEANS
SCRAPED NEW POTATOES (PAGE 47)
COLE SLAW   CRUMB CAKE AND APPLESAUCE

One of the most traditional of all the Pennsylvania Dutch dishes is ham and green beans, cooked together. With potatoes and cole slaw, that's a real farmer's meal.

I prefer to cook the beans separately in the ham broth, so they don't get overdone and soggy. In July, when the sweet corn is in, I sometimes add corn cut off the cob and just heat it through.

People always want to know why our cole slaw tastes different. I think it must be because we squeeze it gently with the vinegar, sugar, and seasonings until everything is blended. It seems to take that raw cabbage taste away.

HAM AND GREEN BEANS

Trim the rind from a 4-pound butt end of home-cured ham. Put in a 3-quart saucepan or Dutch oven, cover with water and cook, covered, over medium heat until tender, about 3 hours. Remove ham.

Add 2 pounds cleaned and trimmed fresh green beans

to the ham broth and cook about 15 minutes, until just tender. Slice the ham and add to the beans.

VARIATION

Add 1 cup corn to the beans and let it heat through.

COLE SLAW

    1 firm head cabbage
    1 green pepper, seeded
    1 red pepper, seeded
    1 cup sugar
    ½ cup cider vinegar
    ½ teaspoon salt
    ½ teaspoon celery seed

Shred the cabbage and peppers. Put in a large bowl; add the sugar, vinegar, salt, and celery seed and press with the hand until all the juices are blended. Chill in the refrigerator for at least 1 hour. A few grated carrots can be added for color and flavor variation.

TO MAKE CREAMED COLE SLAW

Add 1 cup mayonnaise.

CRUMB CAKE

    4 cups flour
    ¾ cup butter
    2½ cups brown sugar
    1 teaspoon cinnamon
    1 teaspoon ground cloves
    2 teaspoons baking soda
    1½ cups buttermilk

Blend the flour, butter, sugar, and spices with a pastry blender or your hands until it makes fine crumbs. Reserve 1½ cups of crumbs for the topping. Dissolve the soda in the buttermilk and mix with remaining crumbs until well blended. Pour into 2 greased 9-inch cake pans and top with the reserved crumbs. Bake in a 350° oven for 35 to 40 minutes. Serve warm, with applesauce.

APPLESAUCE

Peel, core, and slice 2 pounds tart green apples and cook in 1½ cups water on low heat until soft, about 15 minutes. Put through a food mill or sieve. Add 1 cup granulated sugar to the puréed apple (if you use later, sweeter apples, reduce the amount of sugar) and bring to a boil. Boil 2 minutes and serve warm. Garnish, if you like, with a sprinkling of cinnamon or nutmeg.

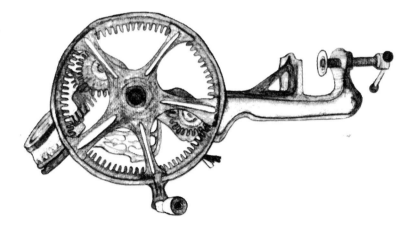

SPRING WEDDING DINNER

FRESH FRUIT CUP   FRENCH TURKEY (FRESH BAKED HAM)
COLD ROLLED BONED RIB ROAST
SCRAPED NEW POTATOES (PAGE 47)   PEAS IN PATTY SHELLS
SPICED CANTALOUPE   CHOW CHOW (PAGES 216 AND 220)
WHITE AND WHOLE WHEAT BREAD (PAGES 182 AND 184)
WEDDING CAKE   VANILLA ICE CREAM (PAGE 77)
OLIVES   SALTED NUTS   PRETZELS   NUT KISSES
CHOCOLATE-COATED CREAMS *or* BUTTER MINTS (PAGE 204)

Weddings are a big event in the Mennonite community. There were 500 people at my wedding; so we had to have two receptions, the first for my family and friends and the second, a month later, for Abe's. Only the immediate family came to both.

Our weddings are held in the morning and after the pictures have been taken and we have all visited a while, we sit down at noon to a full-course dinner at home—never in a restaurant. Nowadays, the young Mennonites prefer a light menu, but with us it was traditional to have just about everything you could think of, which meant hours and hours of preparation and cooking. We had one hot and one cold meat, potatoes and a vegetable, according to season, and always something in patty shells. The first time I remember patty shells was when Aunt Ruth made them for a wedding; the dining room was full of them! One aunt would do one thing; another would do something else, like scraping potatoes, whatever she was best at.

When everyone sat down at table, the fruit cup would be

there on a small plate, all fresh fruits prepared in the fanciest way, balled or cubed. The meat and vegetables were put on the big dinner plates and served individually, with bread and butter and relishes passed at the table. The bride and groom, the "weddners" as they are called in the Pennsylvania Dutch country, would be served first, then the host.

After the main course was finished, the plates and silverware were cleared away and the dessert brought on. We are funny—we never eat olives at the beginning of a meal but at the end, with the ice cream; we just love the salt-and-sweet combination of olives or pretzels with ice cream. Now when I go to a restaurant and the first thing served is the olives, that really tickles me.

FRENCH TURKEY (FRESH BAKED HAM)

Mother always called the baked fresh ham or uncured leg of pork "French turkey." I don't know why, but the name still sticks.

This is roasted in much the same way as any other cut of pork. We remove the rind and place the ham bone side down in a baking dish or roasting pan, add water, and cover the meat lightly with foil.

After removing the rind, salt and pepper the ham generously (use more seasoning than you would think necessary) and place in a roaster pan fat side up. Add 3 cups water and cover the pan with the lid or with heavy foil. Bake at 375° for 4 hours. Remove cover for last 30 minutes to brown meat.

FOR ROAST PORK LOIN

Follow the same method but cook only 3½ hours.

RIB ROAST

For rib roasts, either boned and rolled or bone-in, we season the meat very heavily with salt, all that will stay on, and plenty of pepper. Add ½ inch of water to the roasting pan and cover the meat loosely with foil. Bake a roast under 10 pounds about 2½ hours at 375°. Bake a rib roast with bone weighing from 10 to 25 pounds for 3½ to 4 hours at 400°, also covered with foil. A meat thermometer is helpful in determining when the meat reaches the internal temperature you prefer. In the Pennsylvania Dutch country, people like their beef well done; but for the restaurant we cook our rib roasts fairly rare, though a rolled boned rib roast is always served well done, and often cold.

Note: Save the brown glaze on the bottom of the pan in which the ham or beef was cooked for gravy or broth for stews or soups. Pour off the fat, add several cups of water, and put the pan on medium heat for several minutes to loosen the browning, stirring with a wooden spoon. Use this ham broth to cook green beans (see p. 152).

PEAS IN PATTY SHELLS

⅓ cup butter
¼ teaspoon salt
1 cup flour
¼ cup milk

We use milk, rather than water, when we make patty shells. It makes the pastry richer and it becomes golden brown instead of white.

Cut butter, salt, and flour with a pastry blender until fine, or rub to fine crumbs with the fingers. Slowly add milk with the left hand while tossing the crumbs lightly with the right. When moist, press together to form a ball. Put on a generously floured surface, pat slightly to smooth edges, and roll out about 1/8 inch thick. Cut circles of dough to fit into muffin tins. Press into tins and crimp edges. Prick bottom to prevent pastry rising and puffing. Bake in a 325° oven until golden brown, approximately 15 minutes. This will make 6 patty shells.

PEA FILLING

½ cup water
1 quart fresh garden peas, shelled
1 teaspoon salt
1 teaspoon sugar
1 tablespoon butter
½ cup heavy cream

Bring water to a boil. Add peas, salt, sugar, and butter and boil 2 minutes. Add cream and remove from heat as soon as cream is hot. Pour into patty shells and serve immediately.

NUT KISSES

⅓ cup egg whites
¼ teaspoon cream of tartar
1 cup sifted confectioners' sugar
¼ teaspoon salt
1 cup coarsely broken nutmeats

Beat egg whites with cream of tartar until they form soft peaks. Sift together the sugar and salt and gradually beat into the egg whites. Beat until they hold very stiff peaks. Fold in the nutmeats. Drop mixture by teaspoons onto greased cooky sheets. Bake on the middle rack of a preheated 375° oven, one sheet at a time, until the edges and peaks are very lightly golden, approximately 7 to 8 minutes. Do not overbake; the kisses should be moist inside and dry outside. Cool thoroughly before packing in airtight containers. This makes 24 kisses.

FOUR SUMMER LUNCHEONS

CHICKEN CORN SOUP   COLD SLICED BAKED HAM
POTATO SALAD   APRICOT COBBLER

In our family, soup was not the most favored dish. To us, it was something you ate during the Depression. If we did have a soup, it had to be the kind you could almost eat with a fork, something substantial like potato soup, chicken corn soup, ham and bean soup, or beef vegetable soup; and we didn't eat it from soup plates but on ironstone plates—not completely flat, with a bit of a dip in them. Chicken corn soup is probably one of the best known of all Pennsylvania Dutch soups, and when it is made with good rich chicken broth, corn freshly cut from the cob, and homemade noodles, nothing can be more delicious. The longer it stands, the better it tastes.

CHICKEN CORN SOUP

6 cups rich seasoned chicken broth
2 cups diced cooked chicken
2 cups corn kernels (freshly cut off the cob)
1 cup Homemade Noodles, broken into 1-inch pieces
    (see p. 39)
1 cup chopped celery
2 tablespoons chopped parsley
1 teaspoon salt (depending on seasoning in broth)
¼ teaspoon freshly ground pepper

To give this soup a lot of flavor, cook a chicken in the broth until tender; then remove, skin and debone, and cut into bite-

A cluster of summer fruits and vegetables on the stone steps leading to the tobacco barn.

size pieces. Bring the broth to a boil; add the corn, noodles, celery, parsley, salt, and pepper. Boil 5 minutes; then add the chicken. This can be garnished with slices of hard-boiled egg, if desired.

POTATO SALAD

  2 pounds firm mealy potatoes, such as Irish Cobbler
  4 ribs celery, chopped
  6 hard-boiled eggs, chopped
  2 tablespoons minced parsley
    Dash of Worcestershire sauce
    Hot Bacon Dressing (see p. 35)

Scrub the potatoes, cover with water, and boil until tender. Peel and dice. (The easiest way to do this is to slice the peeled potatoes with a French-fry cutter into even pieces, then dice them.) Combine potatoes, celery, eggs, parsley, Worcestershire sauce, and hot dressing. Cover and let stand in the refrigerator for at least 3 hours.

APRICOT COBBLER

FOR FRUIT MIXTURE	FOR CAKE TOPPING
¾ cup sugar	1 cup flour
1 tablespoon cornstarch	1 tablespoon sugar
1 cup boiling water	1½ teaspoons baking powder
3 cups canned apricot halves	½ teaspoon salt
1 tablespoon butter	3 tablespoons butter
¼ teaspoon cinnamon	½ cup milk
⅛ teaspoon nutmeg	

Dissolve the sugar and cornstarch in the boiling water and boil for 1 minute. Add the apricot halves, butter, and spices and heat through. Spread in a buttered 1½-quart baking dish.

Sift the flour with the sugar, baking powder, and salt. Work in the butter and then stir in the milk, to make a soft dough. Put this over the fruit and bake in a 400° oven for 30 minutes. Serve hot or cold.

TOMATO JUICE (PAGE 222)   CORN PIE
GARDEN SALAD WITH OIL AND VINEGAR *or*
SWEET AND SOUR DRESSING (PAGE 43)
OLD-FASHIONED CHOCOLATE CAKE WITH CARAMEL ICING

You've no idea how good corn can taste when it's baked in a pie. I often make this for lunch and sometimes I add clams, as a variation.

The chocolate cake is the one we serve in the restaurant. Everyone loves it; it's dark, moist, and rich and even better the next day. The recipe, which came from my mother's side of the family, was written down as "two big white cups" of this, "a little" of that, not very exact; and I found out that the less fussy you were about the leveling, the better it came out. One change I did make was to use strong coffee instead of the original boiling water because it enhances the flavor of the cocoa. The caramel icing is very simple and the confectioners' sugar makes it beautifully smooth. I use it on all kinds of cakes.

CORN PIE

4 cups fresh corn, cut off the cob
4 eggs, lightly beaten
1 teaspoon salt
2 teaspoons sugar
  Freshly ground pepper to taste
2 tablespoons flour
½ cup melted butter
  9-inch unbaked pie shell, plus enough extra pastry for a
    top crust

Combine the corn, eggs, salt, sugar, pepper, flour, and butter.
Pour into the pie shell. Cover with the top crust, making a vent
for the steam to escape. Bake in a 350° oven for 1 hour.

VARIATION

For corn-clam pie, add ½ cup chopped raw clams or canned
minced clams to the filling.

OLD-FASHIONED CHOCOLATE CAKE

2 cups brown sugar
½ cup butter
2 eggs
¾ cup buttermilk
½ cup cocoa
½ cup boiling-hot strong coffee
1 teaspoon baking soda
1 teaspoon cider vinegar
½ teaspoon salt
1 teaspoon vanilla
2½ cups sifted all-purpose flour

Cream the sugar, butter, and eggs until fluffy. Mix in the buttermilk. Combine the cocoa and coffee in a saucepan, adding

the liquid very slowly to prevent lumping, then mix into the creamed mixture. Moisten the baking soda with the vinegar and stir in with the salt and vanilla. Gradually beat in the flour, beating until smooth. Pour into a greased and floured 13x9-inch cake pan. Bake in a 350° oven for approximately 45 minutes. Cool. Ice with caramel icing.

CARAMEL ICING

> ½ cup butter
> 1 cup brown sugar
> ¼ cup evaporated milk
> Pinch of salt
> 1¾ to 2 cups confectioners' sugar (enough for a spreading consistency)

Melt butter in a saucepan; add the brown sugar and boil over low heat for 2 minutes, stirring constantly. Add milk and salt and stir until it comes to a full boil. Remove from heat and cool until lukewarm. Gradually beat in the confectioners' sugar, beating until the icing is thick enough to spread.

CHERRY PUDDING *or* APPLE DUMPLINGS
SLICED COLD MEATS

This is the kind of lunch we had on the farm on a very hot day; the combination of fruit and meat was very refreshing, eaten in alternate bites, with ice-cold rich milk or cream poured over the pudding or dumplings. Apple dumplings are especially good with cold ham or pork, the cherry pudding with beef or lamb.

CHERRY PUDDING

2 eggs
2 tablespoons sugar
2 tablespoons butter
2 cups flour
1 teaspoon salt
2 teaspoons baking powder
1 cup milk
2 cups pitted semisweet cherries

Cream the eggs, sugar, and butter until fluffy. Sift the flour, salt, and baking powder together. Add the flour and milk alternately to the creamed mixture, beating until smooth. Fold in 1 cup of the cherries, put in a 9x13-inch cake pan, and bake in a 350° oven for 50 minutes. Serve hot, with the remaining cherries on top and a pitcher of rich milk or cream.

APPLE DUMPLINGS

6 medium baking apples, peeled and cored
½ cup cinnamon hearts (hard candies)
2 cups flour
2½ teaspoons baking powder
½ teaspoon salt
⅔ cup butter
½ cup milk
2 cups brown sugar
2 cups water
⅛ teaspoon cinnamon
⅛ teaspoon nutmeg
⅓ cup butter

Fill the cored center of the apples with the cinnamon hearts. Sift the flour, baking powder, and salt together; then cut in the shortening until mixture is fine and crumbly. Sprinkle the milk over it and press lightly, working the dough only enough to hold together. Roll out dough and cut into 6-inch squares. Place an apple on each and bring dough up around apple to cover it completely. Moisten top edges with water and fasten securely on top of apple. Place dumplings 1 inch apart in a greased baking pan.

Combine the brown sugar, water, and spices in a pan and cook, stirring, for five minutes, until dissolved. Remove from heat and stir in butter. Pour this mixture over the dumplings.

Bake in a 375° oven for 35 to 40 minutes, basting occasionally. Serve hot with chilled rich milk, or, preferably, cream.

FRUIT SOUP   CHICKEN SALAD   ORANGE ICE

Fruit soups are very traditional in our area. We'd have them at noontime in the summer when the men were working and the weather was very hot, or at the evening meal. They were something we always looked forward to. The recipe is so simple people think they aren't going to like it, but like cracker pudding, it tastes better than it sounds. There's a simplicity and beauty about the homemade bread with the berries and sugar and milk, everything absolutely fresh and good; and it isn't soggy, as you might think. We'd present the soup in a pretty bowl or an ironstone tureen, with two pitchers of chilled milk, one plain and one sweetened.

The chicken salad is my mother's recipe; it was one of the cold dishes we served at summer wedding buffets. When I was first married, she gave me her recipe—one crock of chicken, one crock of celery—and I've had to work out the

63

right proportions. We always use a clear white vinegar or cider vinegar in our dressings, not wine vinegar, which wouldn't be right with the sugar, or the type of dressings we make.

The orange ice recipe is simple, too; but it is tart, cool, and refreshing and that little touch of nutmeg makes a whole lot of difference.

FRUIT SOUP

6 cups bread cubes, made from day-old white bread, preferably homemade
4 cups fresh fruit (strawberries, raspberries, blackberries, blueberries, or diced peaches)
1 cup granulated sugar
3 cups chilled milk

Place bread cubes in bowl; add fruit and sugar. Toss lightly. Pour the milk over the fruit just a few minutes before serving.

CHICKEN SALAD

4 cups diced chicken
2 cups chopped celery
8 hard-boiled eggs, chopped

FOR DRESSING

1 cup distilled white vinegar or cider vinegar
1 cup sugar
1 tablespoon prepared mustard
1 cup milk
2 egg yolks
2 tablespoons cornstarch
¼ teaspoon turmeric

Combine the chicken, celery, and eggs in a bowl. Bring the vinegar and sugar to a boil in a saucepan and stir until sugar dissolves. Remove from heat. Mix together the mustard, milk, egg yolks, cornstarch, and turmeric. Mix into the vinegar-sugar mixture with a wire whip, blending well. Cook over medium heat, stirring constantly, until thickened. Pour dressing over salad, and chill. This is best made and served the same day; it tends to get watery if allowed to stand too long.

ORANGE ICE

    1 cup concentrated frozen orange juice
    1 pint 7-Up
    1 pint grapefruit soda or Tom Collins mix, or similar
           tart soda
    Several dashes or gratings of nutmeg

Blend all ingredients, pour into 9x11-inch oblong cake pan, and freeze until firm. Remove from pan and place in sherbet glasses. Serve as a dessert or with hot food.

THREE SUMMER DINNERS

FRIED CHICKEN
SCRAPED NEW POTATOES WITH BROWNED BUTTER (PAGES 47 AND 34)
CORN FRITTERS   CHOW CHOW (PAGE 220)
BLUEBERRY SHORTCAKE

Summer has to be my busiest season in the kitchen. The fields and gardens and the Lancaster County farmers' markets are overflowing with the most beautiful fresh vegetables and fruits you ever saw—and do we make the most of them! In July and August I start canning all the relishes we use in the restaurant, making wine, and freezing berries and corn, peas and lima beans.

I figure I freeze 600 quarts of sweet corn every year. It takes a dozen ears to make a quart; and between 10:00 in the morning and 2:00 in the afternoon, with four helpers, we can cut the kernels off fifty dozen ears. You have to work like lightning. The corn must be picked first thing in the morning when it is full of flavor and blanched the minute it is husked; but if you live in the country it is well worth your while to buy corn when it is in season and cheap and freeze it, because it tastes just like fresh corn. Then you can have corn fritters, corn pudding, or creamed corn any time you feel like it. You'll find my method of blanching, cutting, and freezing corn on page 208, and it's amazing how fast you can do it if everyone in the family pitches in.

66

FRIED CHICKEN

1 cup flour
2 teaspoons salt
¼ teaspoon pepper
½ teaspoon celery salt
1 teaspoon paprika
2 frying chickens, cut in serving pieces
½ cup shortening (preferably butter) for frying

Combine the flour, salt, pepper, celery salt, and paprika in a brown paper bag. Add chicken pieces and shake until fully coated. Melt shortening in a heavy skillet (the black iron kind is ideal) and put in chicken, skin side down. Cook until golden brown on both sides; then cover and cook over low heat until tender—about 40 minutes. For a crisp crust, uncover the skillet for the last 5 or 10 minutes.

CORN FRITTERS

2 cups corn kernels, cut off the cob
1 teaspoon salt
½ teaspoon sugar
2 tablespoons flour
⅛ teaspoon freshly ground pepper
2 eggs, lightly beaten
Shortening for frying (preferably butter)

This is very easy if you put all the ingredients, except the shortening, in the blender and whirl them until well mixed. Heat the shortening in a heavy skillet and drop the corn mixture into the hot fat by tablespoons. Fry on each side until golden brown. Serve, if you like, with molasses or syrup.

BLUEBERRY SHORTCAKE

Follow directions for Strawberry Shortcake (see p. 48), substituting sugared whole blueberries for the strawberries.

PORK POT PIE   BROILED TOMATO HALVES
BANANA CAKE WITH BUTTER CREAM FROSTING

Pot pie, squares of dough cooked in broth with vegetables and meat, is a real staple Pennsylvania Dutch one-dish meal, something that everyone in the family enjoys eating and the children love to help you with by picking up the little squares of rolled-out dough and dropping them in the pot. You can use just about any kind of meat—pork, beef, chicken, or if you have a hunter in the family, pheasant or squirrel.

This was a favorite of our adopted son, Bob Rote. He could eat twice as much pot pie as anyone else in the family and he liked to pick out the thick, doughy pieces that had stuck together in the cooking. Now Bob's little girl, Sherry, loves to help me roll out the dough when she comes to see us.

The Berks County Dutch have another version of pot pie that's made with apples cooked in plenty of water with brown sugar until they get soft like applesauce, with the dough cooked on top.

Pot pie is pretty filling; so you don't need much with it except a vegetable. The broiled tomato recipe comes from Mrs. Martha Barr, a friend of mine, and it's just delicious.

PORK POT PIE

6-pound pork loin or shoulder roast
6 cups pork or chicken broth
2 stalks celery, coarsely chopped
2 medium-sized potatoes, peeled and thinly sliced

POT PIE DOUGH

2½ cups flour
 2 eggs
⅓ cup water
 1 tablespoon butter
½ teaspoon salt

Cook the pork loin according to the recipe for Pork Pot Roast (see p. 84). When cooked, cut the meat in small pieces and keep warm.

You need a very heavy pot, such as a Dutch oven or 6-quart enameled cast-iron casserole to cook the pot pie. Put the broth, celery, and potatoes in the pot, plus salt if the broth is not well seasoned, and simmer for 10 minutes.

Mound the flour on a pastry board or marble slab and make a well in the center. Break the eggs into the well and add the water, butter, and salt. Gradually mix the flour into the other ingredients until well blended. Gather into a ball and knead the dough until it is very tender, smooth, and elastic.

Generously flour the board and roll out the dough very thin—no more than ⅛ inch thick; the thinner you roll it, the more delicate it will be. Cut in 2-inch squares.

Bring the broth and vegetables to a boil over high heat. Drop the pot pie squares into the broth in layers, being careful not to put in a second layer until the boiling broth has covered the first one. As the pot gets full, take a fork and push the squares down. Cook until the squares are tender, about 10 to 12 minutes; then add the pieces of pork, cover, and simmer · for 5 minutes, until heated through. Serve the pot pie, meat, and broth in bowls.

BROILED TOMATO HALVES

Peel 6 firm ripe tomatoes and halve crosswise. Roll in flour, dip in melted butter, and sprinkle each top with ½ teaspoon brown sugar and a little salt and pepper. Broil 5 minutes, or until golden brown.

BANANA CAKE

¼ cup butter
½ cup vegetable shortening
1 cup sugar
2 eggs, well beaten
1 teaspoon vanilla
2 cups cake flour
½ teaspoon salt
⅔ teaspoon baking soda
5 tablespoons buttermilk or sour milk
1 cup banana pulp
Butter Cream Frosting (see opposite)

Cream the butter and shortening. Add the sugar, and cream together until light and fluffy. Add the beaten eggs and vanilla and mix thoroughly. Sift the flour; measure and sift again with the salt. Dissolve the baking soda in the buttermilk.

Add the dry ingredients and buttermilk alternately to the creamed mixture, beating thoroughly after each addition. Fold in the banana pulp until well blended. Pour batter into 2 greased and floured 8-inch layer cake pans and bake in a 350° oven for 30 minutes. This makes a very moist and delicious cake. Cool and ice with Butter Cream Frosting.

BUTTER CREAM FROSTING

1 pound confectioners' sugar
3 tablespoons butter
¼ cup evaporated milk
¼ teaspoon salt

Cream the sugar and butter together and mix in the evaporated milk and salt.

ORANGE ICE CUBES IN 7-UP   BROILED CHICKEN
SCRAPED NEW POTATOES WITH CREAM   CORN ON THE COB
FRENCH-FRIED EGGPLANT   SLICED TOMATOES
BLUEBERRY CRUMB PIE WITH VANILLA ICE CREAM

This is a rather more elaborate chicken dinner than the first, good for company. The orange ice in 7-Up is a very refreshing start to the meal. Freeze the orange ice mixture on page 65 (or, if you prefer, fresh orange juice) in ice cube trays; then drop two or three cubes in a tall glass or goblet, fill with 7-Up, and garnish with a sprig of mint.

The chicken recipe is one I picked up from Fanny Riehl, an Amish girl I had working for me. It's the easiest thing to do, sort of a cross between broiling and frying, and a great favorite in the restaurant. All that butter gives the chicken a wonderful flavor and moistness and it gets real crisp.

My aunt Ruth taught me how to make pies when I was

71

so little I had to stand on a stool to reach the tabletop. She had the patience to explain each step, tell me what I should learn first, what I shouldn't do, and how it should come out. It was really a ceremony, as she stood there and slowly dribbled the ice water on the pie crumbs. She always told me, "Don't play with the dough. The less you handle it, the better it will be." That has always stuck in my mind and I say it to everyone I teach how to make a flaky crust.

We always use a combination of butter and good lard for our shortening (vegetable shortening is not as satisfactory as lard; it tends to make the dough tougher). It is this that gives our pie pastry the delicacy, flakiness, and nuttiness everyone remarks on.

There are a few other hints I learned along the way. You can make a large quantity of the pie-dough crumbs, then save them in a gallon jar in the refrigerator and take some out whenever you want to make a pie. This has been a big help to me. I make enough crumbs for 25 pies at a time. A lot of people find it difficult or a bother to make just one piecrust at a time; but if you have the crumbs on hand, all you have to do is add the water and you can have a fresh pie every day with no problem at all.

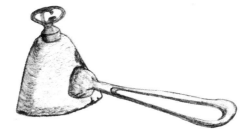

BROILED CHICKEN

½ cup butter
3 frying chickens, cut in serving pieces
2 teaspoons salt
½ teaspoon freshly ground pepper

Melt the butter in the broiler pan (remove the rack), so that you have a layer of butter about ¼ inch deep. Lay the chicken pieces in the butter, lightly salting and peppering them, with the bone side up. Broil until golden brown, turn, season the skin side, and broil until golden brown. Reduce oven heat to 350° and bake chicken for 15 minutes.

SCRAPED NEW POTATOES WITH CREAM

Boil scraped potatoes according to directions for Scraped New Potatoes on p. 47. Drain, put in a serving dish, and pour heated heavy cream over them.

CORN ON THE COB

Allow 2 ears of freshly picked corn per person, or more according to appetites. Husk and silk the corn, clean, and rinse. Put in a large pot and cover with *cold* water. Cover pot and quickly bring water to a boil; then boil corn exactly 3 minutes, no longer, or until no milk oozes from the kernels when you pierce them with a fork. Do not overcook or the corn will be tough. Brush with melted butter, or let guests butter their own.

FRENCH-FRIED EGGPLANT

    1 large eggplant
    2 eggs, beaten
    1 cup bread crumbs
      Fat or oil for frying
      Salt

Peel eggplant and cut into ¼-inch-thick slices; then cut into long thick strips with a French-fry cutter. Dip strips in beaten egg, then in bread crumbs. If possible, chill about 30 minutes so the coating adheres.

Heat fat to 375°. (Drop a cube of bread into the fat. If it browns quickly, the fat is hot enough; so turn it from high to medium heat.) Fry eggplant in the same way as French-fried potatoes. Drain on paper towels and sprinkle with salt.

If you prefer, just slice the eggplant, egg and crumb it, and fry in fat or oil in a skillet until golden brown on each side.

BLUEBERRY CRUMB PIE

BASIC PIE DOUGH (enough for 3 9-inch pie shells)

    ⅔ cup lard
    ⅓ cup butter
    1 teaspoon salt
    3 cups all-purpose flour
    ½ cup (approximately) ice water

Cut or rub the lard, butter, and salt into the flour until it makes fine crumbs, about the size of seed pearls. Carefully dribble the ice water over the crumbs with your left hand while tossing the crumbs lightly with your right hand. Use only enough water to keep the dough together and make sure it does not all hit the same spot. As the dough becomes moist, gently press it to the side of the bowl.

Take only as much dough as you need for the size of pan you are using. Form the remainder into a ball, cover tightly with plastic wrap, and refrigerate (or roll out, fit into pie pans, cover with plastic wrap and freeze, if you are not going to use it right away).

Put the amount of dough you are using onto a generously floured board or marble slab. Gently pat it into a ball; then flatten the ball lightly, patting the edges so there are no rough, dry sides.

Roll out the dough about ⅛-inch thick, moving the rolling pin first north and south, then east and west. If the circle is not quite round, roll one time in between—northeast to southwest. When you have a nice even round circle about an inch larger than your pie pan, place the dough in the pan, cut off excess dough and crimp the edge. Keep the pieces of excess dough in plastic wrap and roll them out on a cooky sheet to make pastry squares for Chicken Stoltzfus (see p. 151), but don't try to use the dough over and over again or it will get very tough. Just form them into one ball and roll them out. Cut with a pastry wheel or pizza cutter.

Leftover dough can also be used for snails; butter it, sprinkle with cinnamon or spread with jelly, and roll up like a jelly roll. Cut in ½-inch slices and bake in a 350° oven for 15 minutes. Serve plain, buttered, or with butter icing on top. Children love these.

To make a large quantity of pie-dough crumbs, increase the recipe, without adding the ice water. Keep the crumbs in the refrigerator in a screw-topped jar and take out just enough to make a pie (1½ cups crumbs for a 9-inch pie shell), adding the water as before.

You can do the same thing with the following crumb

topping for pies. The crumbs keep well in the refrigerator and save you so much time when you want to make a pie in a hurry.

CRUMB TOPPING (enough for 4 9-inch pies)

    3 cups flour
    ¾ cup butter
    ½ cup granulated sugar

Cut ingredients with a pastry blender or mix with the fingers until very fine.

BLUEBERRY FILLING

    3 tablespoons arrowroot
    ½ cup water
    1 cup sugar
    1 teaspoon lemon juice
      A little grated nutmeg
    2½ cups blueberries
      Unbaked 9-inch pie shell

Dissolve the arrowroot in the water, making a paste. Mix with the sugar in a pan and bring to a boil, stirring until sugar is dissolved and glaze slightly thickened. (Arrowroot is expensive, but it makes a much clearer, finer glaze than cornstarch, which tends to be gummy.) Remove from heat and stir in lemon juice and nutmeg. Fold in the berries.

Pour berries into unbaked 9-inch pie shell and sprinkle with a ½-inch-thick layer of crumb topping. Bake in a 350° oven for 45 minutes. Serve warm or cold, but not straight from the oven or the pie will be hard to cut.

VANILLA ICE CREAM

  5 eggs
  4 cups sugar
½ teaspoon salt
  3 13-ounce cans evaporated milk
  1 pint heavy cream
  4 cups milk
  2 tablespoons vanilla

Cream the eggs, sugar, and salt until fluffy. Mix in the evaporated milk, cream, milk, and vanilla. Pour this into the freezer can of a 6-quart ice cream freezer packed with crushed ice and rock salt, and freeze according to the directions given with your freezer, electric or hand-operated.

A fall harvest of keeping foods:
dried beef and home-cured ham,
dried corn and dried apples,
black walnuts and shellbarks.

TWO FALL LUNCHEONS OR SUPPERS

BROILED SPARERIBS   STIRABOUT

This is a simple, hearty noontime meal we'd have had on the farm when the weather started turning cold, but, while my parents liked to fry the ribs, either pork or beef, I prefer mine broiled. My mother's recipe for stirabout (which is defined in the dictionary as a thick porridge) is very old and traditional, typically Pennsylvania Dutch in the combination of potatoes, chicken broth, saffron, celery, parsley, and knepp, which are tiny batter dumplings, like the rivvels we put in soup. It's important to keep the chicken fat on the broth so the knepp don't stick together. Stirabout is a delicate kind of dish, good with the fatty spareribs.

BROILED SPARERIBS

   3 pounds pork or beef spareribs
   Salt, freshly ground pepper, other herbs of your choice

Season the ribs with salt, pepper, and any other seasoning or herb you like to use on them. Broil on both sides until the meat is well done, brown, and crisp (beef will take longer than pork). Drain on paper towels and serve very hot.

STIRABOUT

```
 2  pounds white potatoes
1½  quarts rich chicken broth, with fat
 2  large stems celery, chopped
 1  tablespoon chopped parsley or parsley flakes
    A pinch of saffron
⅛  teaspoon freshly ground pepper
 2  eggs
½  cup flour
```

Peel the potatoes and cut in ¼-inch-thick slices. Bring the broth to a boil in a large pot and put in the potatoes, celery, parsley, and seasonings (taste broth and add salt, if needed). Make the knepp by beating the eggs and flour with a fork to a thin paste. Drop this into the boiling broth with the tip of a spoon, about ½ teaspoon at a time. When all the knepp are in, continue to cook at a full boil for 7 minutes.

NOODLES WITH CHICKEN AND BROWNED BUTTER
MASHED POTATOES (PAGE 45)   FRIED TOMATOES
MONTGOMERY PIE

It is not unusual for us to have two starchy dishes at one meal, for we dearly love our noodles and potatoes. The Pennsylvania Dutch way of frying tomatoes is one you should try; the brown sugar caramelizes and gives a wonderful flavor and the tomatoes draw a lot of juice which combines with the butter and is just wonderful poured over mashed potatoes. The secret is in having firm tomatoes that won't fall apart.

Montgomery pie is really the Philadelphia version of shoofly pie, a bit more elegant. When you make it, the bottom is the cake and the top is the gooey part, but when it is baked it reverses itself; the cake is on the top and the goo on the bottom.

NOODLES WITH CHICKEN
AND BROWNED BUTTER

Make the noodles according to the directions for Homemade Noodles on page 39. Cook uncovered in plenty of rapidly boiling salted water, adding 1 tablespoon oil or butter, until tender, about 15 minutes. Drain well. Add to the noodles 3 cups leftover boiled chicken, diced, and 4 tablespoons Browned Butter (see p. 34) and toss well.

FRIED TOMATOES

8 firm unpeeled tomatoes
1 cup flour
4 tablespoons butter or shortening
1 teaspoon salt
⅛ cup brown sugar
⅛ cup granulated sugar

Slice the tomatoes ¼ inch thick and flour on both sides. Melt the butter or shortening in a heavy skillet and fry the tomatoes until golden on one side, salt lightly, turn, and fry the other side. Sprinkle with the combined brown and granulated sugars and let stand until ready to serve—but not more than 15 minutes or they will lose their shape.

MONTGOMERY PIE

2 unbaked 9-inch pie shells

TOP PART

    Grated rind of 1 lemon
½ cup sugar
½ cup molasses
 1 egg, beaten
 1 tablespoon flour
 1 cup boiling water

Blend all ingredients in a saucepan and bring to a boil.

BOTTOM PART

   1 cup sugar
 ¼ cup lard or shortening
   1 egg
 ½ cup milk
1½ cups flour
  2 teaspoons baking powder
 ½ teaspoon salt

Cream the sugar and shortening in a mixer; then beat in the egg. Beat in the milk, alternately with the flour sifted with baking powder and salt. Pour this into the unbaked pie shells, dividing it evenly; then pour on the topping. Bake in a 350° oven for 45 minutes.

THREE FALL DINNERS

PORK POT ROAST   TURNIPS AND POTATOES
BUTTERED SPINACH   APPLE PIE WITH ICE CREAM

Although everyone knows beef pot roast, not everyone knows how good a pork pot roast can be. We take the rich broth from the cooked meat and boil turnips and potatoes in it.

When I do spinach, I barely cook it, just bring it to a boil with only the water clinging to the leaves and then take it off the heat. Most of my vegetables are seasoned with salt and sugar; the sugar seems to bring out the true, earthy flavor. With browned butter poured over them, who could ask for anything more?

PORK POT ROAST

Rub a 3-pound pork loin, the large end with the bone in, with 1½ teaspoons salt and ½ teaspoon freshly ground pepper. Put in a heavy 3-quart kettle or Dutch oven with 4 cups water, or just enough to cover. Bring to a boil, reduce heat to a simmer, cover, and cook over low heat for 2 hours.

Before serving, remove the pork and put it under the broiler just long enough to brown the fat. Measure 2 cups of the broth and reserve for the turnips and potatoes.

TURNIPS AND POTATOES

1½ pounds turnips
1½ pounds potatoes
 2 cups pork broth
 1 teaspoon salt
 ⅛ teaspoon freshly ground pepper
 2 teaspoons chopped chives

Peel turnips and potatoes and slice ⅓ inch thick. Put in a pan with the broth and seasonings and bring to a boil. Boil 20 minutes. Serve in the broth, which can be mashed into the vegetables.

BUTTERED SPINACH

1½ pounds fresh spinach
 1 teaspoon salt
 ½ teaspoon sugar
 2 tablespoons Browned Butter (see p. 34)

Clean the spinach, removing tough stalks, and wash thoroughly. Shake lightly so there is still some water clinging to the leaves. Put spinach, salt, and sugar in a saucepan, cover, and bring to a boil. Stir once; then remove from heat and let stand until ready to serve. Drain well and toss with Browned Butter.

APPLE PIE

    1 unbaked 9-inch pie shell and enough pie dough for
          top crust
    3½ cups peeled, cored, and sliced tart apples
    ¾ cup sugar
    ¼ teaspoon cinnamon
       Dash of nutmeg
    ¼ teaspoon salt
    2 teaspoons lemon juice
       A little grated lemon rind
    1 tablespoon butter

Fill the pie shell with the apples. Mix the sugar, spices, salt, lemon juice and rind and sprinkle over apples. Dot with the butter. Moisten edges of the pie shell with water, cover with the top crust, and seal. Make cuts in the top for the steam to escape. Bake in a 375° oven for 50 minutes. Serve warm or cold.

FRIED LIVER   MASHED POTATOES (page 45)
DAD'S FAVORITE LIMA BEANS   PEPPER RELISH (page 219)
LEMON MERINGUE PIE

Mother used to say that if you have meat, potatoes, a vegetable, a sour, and fruit or a pie, you have a good meal. Because Dad had the butcher shop, we always built our meals around meat; we had it morning, noon, and night.

Lima beans were one of my Dad's favorite vegetables, and this is his favorite way of doing them. The very best lima beans are the pole limas, next best are the Fordhook; the baby lima, as far as I'm concerned, is hardly worth buying.

FRIED LIVER

     2 pounds liver, sliced 1 inch thick
    ½ cup flour
     3 tablespoons butter
        Salt, freshly ground black pepper

Dust both sides of the liver with the flour. Heat the butter in a heavy skillet, add the liver slices, and sprinkle lightly with salt and pepper. Fry until golden brown; turn over and fry on the other side. This should take no more than 10 minutes. The faster liver is cooked, the tenderer it will be.

If you like fried onions with your liver, cook them in the skillet first; then remove them and fry the liver.

DAD'S FAVORITE LIMA BEANS

1 quart fresh or frozen lima beans
½ cup water
1 teaspoon salt
1 teaspoon sugar
1 tablespoon butter
1 cup light cream
1 tablespoon Browned Butter (See p. 34)

Put the lima beans in a saucepan with the water, salt, sugar, and butter. Boil until tender, not more than 5 minutes. Remove from heat. Add the cream and just heat through over low heat. Put in a serving dish with the browned butter on top.

LEMON MERINGUE PIE

2 cups water
4 tablespoons cornstarch
1 cup sugar
3 eggs, separated
   Grated rind and juice of 2 lemons
1 tablespoon butter
¼ teaspoon salt
1 baked 9-inch pie shell
¼ teaspoon cream of tartar
4 tablespoons sugar

Mix ½ cup of the water with the cornstarch to make a thin paste. Put the 1 cup sugar and remaining water in a pan and bring to a boil. Add the cornstarch paste and cook until mixture begins to thicken, stirring.

Transfer mixture to a double boiler and cook over hot water for 15 minutes; then pour some of the mixture over the 3 egg yolks, which have been slightly beaten in a bowl. Stir this into the mixture in the top of the double boiler and cook 1 minute. Add lemon rind and juice, butter, and salt. Blend well. Cool mixture and pour into the baked pie shell.

Beat the egg whites with the cream of tartar to the soft-peak stage. Gradually beat in the 4 tablespoons sugar and continue beating until stiff and glossy. Pile this meringue lightly over the pie filling and bake in a 350° oven until meringue is golden brown.

BROWNED CREAMED DRIED BEEF
SWEET POTATO TAILS *or* POTATOES IN THEIR JACKETS (PAGE 42)
or PANCAKES   PICKLED CAULIFLOWER (PAGE 218)
MUSTARD PICKLES (PAGE 217)   WATERMELON *or* HONEYDEW MELON

This was a typical fall dinner for us, because smoked dried beef is a specialty of our part of the country and we always had some in the smokehouse. Smoked dried beef has a lot of flavor, but if you can't get it you could substitute chipped beef or corned beef, though they won't be quite as tasty.

The brown flour paste, which is like the French brown roux, is very important in our cooking, just about as important as browned butter. It's a must for brown potato soup, for tomato sauce, and for the creamy gravy that goes with the dried beef; it's a no-fail method. If you put uncooked flour in with the beef and brown it, often it goes lumpy. When I was young and went to other people's houses, I had a hard time learning to iike chipped beef on toast because for me it should have had a brown flour sauce.

Sweet potato tails are the tiny potatoes you find when you dig sweet potatoes in late September, before the frost. They are no bigger than your little finger and so sweet and good. They won't store; so, rather than throw them away, we boil and eat them. White potatoes, boiled in their jackets, would also be fine with the beef, or you could serve it on toast or over pancakes.

BROWNED CREAMED DRIED BEEF

½ cup butter
½ cup flour
4 cups milk
2 cups cream
½ pound smoked dried beef, very thinly sliced
  Salt, freshly ground pepper

BROWN FLOUR METHOD

Melt the butter in a heavy skillet(an iron one is good for this) and stir in the flour with a wooden spoon. Cook over medium-low heat, stirring constantly, until it turns golden brown. Experiment with the degree of brownness you like. Some like it light, some medium, some dark.

When the flour is browned, gradually add the milk and cream and stir until smooth and creamy. Add the dried beef and simmer on low heat for 5 minutes. Taste for seasoning. The amount of salt you need depends on the saltiness of the beef.

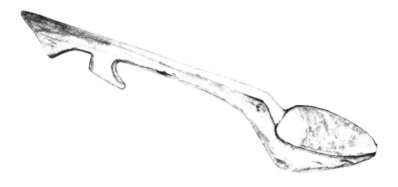

A FALL COMPANY DINNER

FRESH FRUIT CUP
HOT ROLLED RIB ROAST WITH GRAVY (PAGE 54)
FRIED SWEET POTATOES
DAD'S FAVORITE LIMA BEANS (PAGE 88)   BUTTERED CORN
BREAD FILLING (PAGE 104) *or* POTATO FILLING
CELERY HEARTS
CHOW CHOW   SPICED CANTALOUPE   SEVEN-DAY PICKLES
(PAGES 220, 216, AND 218)
CHEESE AND CRACKERS
CRACKER PUDDING   HOME-CANNED PEACHES (PAGE 214)
OLD-FASHIONED CHOCOLATE CAKE WITH CARAMEL ICING (PAGE 60)
COCONUT LAYER CAKE WITH BOILED FROSTING
ANGEL CAKE WITH ICE CREAM   NUT KISSES (PAGE 55)
SALTED NUTS   PRETZELS   HOMEMADE POTATO CHIPS (PAGE 201)
OLIVES   CANDY (CHOCOLATE-COATED CREAMS)   COFFEE

In our group it was sort of the custom to do all your entertaining in spring and fall, right after housecleaning. It just seemed that was the let-up season on the farm, when you could sit back and spend more time baking and cooking. Usually we would entertain twice a week, for eighteen or twenty at a time. On a Saturday the dinner would be in the early evening, or on Sunday, at noontime, and anyone who wanted to stay on could have whatever was left over for supper; there was always plenty. We left the cheese and crackers and cakes on the table and didn't even bother to take them off.

When you had company, you'd really "hang on the agony," as Daddy would say—that's an expression of ours that means put on a show—because nothing was too good for your guests. You could spend a whole week getting ready, polishing the silver and washing your best dishes. It was so much fun, and the table looked really lovely, with relishes in cut-glass dishes and young hearts of homegrown bleached celery arranged in celery glasses or goblets. The home-canned peaches were the big yellow Elberta ones, or the white Champions, and the nut kisses were put on a high silver compote. Then we'd have all kinds of cakes—chocolate and layer cake and angel cake, which is very traditional with us, I think because it is such a good and thrifty way to use up the egg whites after you've made noodles with the yolks.

FRIED SWEET POTATOES

Wash medium-sized sweet potatoes, allowing one per serving. Boil whole in salted water to cover until soft. Drain, cool, and peel. Fry them whole or sliced in half (this way they don't fall apart) in butter in a heavy skillet until golden brown on all sides.

BUTTERED CORN

    4 cups fresh or frozen corn kernels
    ½ cup water
    1 teaspoon salt
    1 teaspoon sugar
    1 tablespoon butter
    2 tablespoons Browned Butter (see p. 34)

Bring corn to a boil in water with salt, sugar, and butter. Boil 3 minutes. Remove from heat, drain, and put in a serving dish. Pour the Browned Butter over the corn.

POTATO FILLING

¾ cup chopped celery and leaves
½ cup boiling water
½ teaspoon salt
¼ teaspoon freshly ground pepper
1 tablespoon chopped parsley
  Pinch of saffron
2 cups mashed potatoes
2 eggs, beaten
2 cups bread cubes
1 cup milk
  Butter

Cook the celery in the water with the salt, pepper, parsley, and saffron until soft, about 10 minutes. Lightly mix with the potatoes, eggs, bread cubes, and milk. Spoon into a well-buttered casserole, dot the top with butter, and bake in a 350° oven for 40 minutes.

CRACKER PUDDING

1 quart milk
2 eggs, separated
⅔ cup granulated sugar
2 cups broken-up saltine crackers
1 cup grated coconut, medium shred
1 teaspoon vanilla

Heat the milk. Beat the egg yolks and sugar until frothy and light. Add to the hot milk, and stir in the crackers and coconut. Cook over medium heat until thick. Remove from heat. Stiffly beat the egg whites and fold in with the vanilla. Serve cool or cold.

COCONUT LAYER CAKE

2½ cups sifted cake flour
2¼ teaspoons baking powder
½ teaspoon salt
⅔ cup butter and lard
1 cup sugar
3 eggs, separated
⅓ cup milk
1 teaspoon vanilla
    Boiled Frosting (see below)
1½ cups shredded coconut

Measure the flour; then add the baking powder and salt and sift three times. Cream the shortening; then gradually beat in the sugar, creaming until very light. Add the egg yolks one by one, beating well after each addition; then beat in the flour mixture alternately with the milk. Beat until smooth. Mix in the vanilla. Stiffly beat the egg whites and fold in. Pour the cake batter into 2 greased and floured 9-inch layer cake pans and bake in a 375° oven for approximately 30 minutes. Remove and cool on racks. Frost and put layers together with Boiled Frosting, and press the coconut over the top and sides of the cake.

BOILED FROSTING

1½ cups sugar
½ cup water
⅛ teaspoon cream of tartar
2 egg whites
½ teaspoon vanilla

Combine the sugar, water, and cream of tartar in a saucepan; stir until dissolved and bring to a boil.

Beat the egg whites, and while doing so, beat in 3 tablespoons of the hot syrup, 1 tablespoon at a time. Meanwhile boil the remaining syrup to 240° on a candy thermometer. Pour this gradually over the egg whites, continuing to beat steadily until the frosting stands in soft peaks; then add the vanilla.

ANGEL CAKE

  1 cup sifted cake flour
¼ teaspoon salt
  1 cup egg whites
¾ teaspoon cream of tartar
  1 cup (scant) granulated sugar
  1 teaspoon vanilla (preferably white) or almond extract

Sift the flour with the salt and measure. Whip the egg whites with the cream of tartar until they hold soft peaks; then fold in the sifted flour and the sugar alternately, 2 tablespoons at a time. Mix in the vanilla or almond extract.

Spoon into a spring-form angel cake pan and bake in a 375° oven for 45 minutes.

FALL WEDDING DINNER

FRESH FRUIT CUP   FRIED OYSTERS   COLD SLICED ROAST BEEF
CHICKEN AND MUSHROOMS IN PATTY SHELLS
SWEET POTATO CROQUETTES   LIMA BEANS
BUTTERED CORN (PAGE 93)   PICKLED RED BEET EGGS
MOTHER'S GOLD CAKE   WHITE CAKE
VANILLA ICE CREAM (PAGE 77)
OLIVES   SALTED NUTS   PRETZELS   NUT KISSES (PAGE 55)
CHOCOLATE-COATED CREAMS *or* BUTTER MINTS (PAGE 204)

A fall wedding dinner followed the same pattern as a spring one, except that some of the foods changed with the seasons; we'd usually have fried oysters then, chicken and mushrooms in patty shells, instead of peas, and sweet potato croquettes, which could be made ahead of time and frozen.

Baking in our region, and in our family, is very competitive. Everyone knew that my father's family were very good cooks; and when my mother moved in, her specialty was this gold cake, for which everyone wanted the recipe. It's a beautiful cake.

FRIED OYSTERS

Allow 4 oysters per serving. Roll them in fresh bread crumbs; then dip in beaten egg and roll again in fresh bread crumbs. Salt lightly on one side. Pan-fry in hot oil until golden brown, about 3 minutes a side.

CHICKEN AND MUSHROOMS IN PATTY SHELLS

⅓ cup arrowroot
⅓ cup water
 3 cups rich chicken stock
 1 cup sliced mushrooms
 1 tablespoon chopped parsley
 4 cups diced cooked chicken
   Patty Shells (see p. 54)

Mix arrowroot and water to a smooth paste. Bring chicken stock to a boil, add parsley and mushrooms, and cook until mushrooms are tender, about 5 minutes. Stir in arrowroot paste and cook, stirring, until thickened. Mix in the chicken. Spoon mixture into the baked patty shells and garnish with parsley sprigs.

SWEET POTATO CROQUETTES

 1 pound sweet potatoes
 1 teaspoon salt
 1 egg, slightly beaten
 2 tablespoons brown sugar
 4 tablespoons butter
   Dry bread crumbs and beaten egg
   Butter or shortening for frying

Boil unpeeled potatoes in salted water to cover until tender. Peel and mash by putting through a food mill, or purée in a blender. Add beaten egg, sugar, and butter, blending well. Chill mixture.

Form into balls, logs, cones, rectangles ½ inch thick and 3 inches long, or whatever shape you fancy. Roll croquettes in bread crumbs, dip in beaten egg, and roll again in crumbs.

Chill a little so coating adheres; then fry in a heavy skillet in butter or shortening until golden brown on all sides. Serve plain, or with mushroom sauce or gravy.

You can make these ahead of time and freeze them. If you do, remove them from the freezer and fry in deep 375° fat until golden brown, drain on paper towels, then place in a 350° oven for 15 minutes.

PICKLED RED BEET EGGS

    1 pound small firm beets, about 2 inches in diameter
    1 cup sugar
  ⅓ cup cider vinegar
    6 hard-boiled eggs, peeled and cooled

Wash and scrub beets and cook in boiling water to cover on low heat until tender, approximately 30 minutes. Remove beets, peel, and slice ¼ inch thick.

Add sugar and vinegar to beet juices in pan. Stir until dissolved and bring to a boil. Add sliced beets and cook on low heat for 5 minutes. Remove beets and strain juice into a bowl or jar. Put in eggs, making sure they are completely covered, and place beets on top of them. Let stand, covered in the refrigerator for at least 12 hours. Serve eggs whole or sliced lengthwise, with sliced beets, as a relish.

MOTHER'S GOLD CAKE

2½ cups sifted cake flour
4 teaspoons baking powder
¾ cup butter
1¼ cups sugar
8 egg yolks, beaten until light
½ teaspoon lemon extract
¾ cup milk
Boiled Frosting (see p. 95)

Measure the flour, add baking powder, and sift again. Cream the butter thoroughly; then gradually beat in the sugar, creaming until light and fluffy. Add the egg yolks and beat well. Add the lemon extract. Beat in the sifted flour and milk alternately, a little at a time, beating until smooth after each addition. Pour or spoon into 3 buttered and floured 8-inch layer cake pans and bake in a 350° oven for 25 minutes. Cool. Put layers together and ice with Boiled Frosting.

WHITE CAKE

4 egg whites
1 cup sugar
⅓ cup butter
1¾ cups cake flour
¼ teaspoon salt
3 teaspoons baking powder
½ cup milk
½ teaspoon vanilla
Caramel Icing (see p. 61)

Beat the egg whites until fluffy. Gradually beat in ½ cup sugar and beat until they hold firm peaks.

Cream the butter and beat in the remaining ½ cup sugar, creaming until light. Sift together the flour, salt, and baking powder. Beat the dry ingredients and the milk alternately into the butter-sugar mixture, beating well after each addition. Fold in the egg whites and the vanilla. Pour into a greased and floured 9 x 13-inch cake pan and bake in a 350° oven for 30 minutes. Cool. Ice with Caramel Icing.

THANKSGIVING DINNER

MUSHROOM SOUP   ROAST TURKEY WITH BREAD FILLING
MASHED POTATOES (PAGE 45)   GIBLET GRAVY   GARDEN PEAS (PAGE 43)
DRIED CORN IN CREAM   CRANBERRY SLUSH
PUMPKIN CHIFFON PIE

In my family, we would never think of roasting any kind of bird without stuffing it with bread filling and having an extra casserole of it. Bread filling, which is second only to potatoes for those of us who love our starchy, buttery foods, is typical of Lancaster County. In Berks County they make their filling with potatoes as well as bread; so it is almost a meal in itself. The secret of a good bread filling is to keep it very rich and moist. Don't be skimpy with the eggs, milk, and butter. When Erma bakes it for the restaurant, she uses butter like it's going out of style—butter on the bottom of the pan, butter dotted all over the top—but I always tell her to be generous; a little is good and a little more can't hurt.

Dried corn is one of the oldest of our traditional foods. We used to dry our own; now we buy it. My mother soaked the dried corn in milk, not water. None of the directions tell you this, but it makes all the difference. It becomes very mild and creamy, not chewy.

I never cared much for pumpkin pie, because it was too heavy and spicy for my taste, but everyone in the restaurant expected pumpkin pie in the fall; so I had to figure out a different filling. I combined two or three recipes and came up with this one, light and subtle, with a custardy bottom and a fluffy top.

MUSHROOM SOUP

1 pound mushrooms, very thinly sliced
6 tablespoons butter
   Salt, freshly ground pepper
6 cups light cream

Mushrooms are best if you don't peel them; just wipe off any dirt with a damp cloth. Melt the butter in a heavy pan and lightly sauté the mushrooms until they are just golden brown. Season with salt and pepper to taste, pour on the light cream, and simmer gently for 10 minutes. Taste for seasoning. Serve very hot.

ROAST TURKEY

9-pound oven-ready turkey
Salt, freshly ground pepper

Rinse turkey, removing giblets. Lightly salt and pepper the inside of the bird. Put giblets in a pan with water to cover, salt, and pepper. Bring to a boil and simmer until soft.

BREAD FILLING

8 cups bread cubes
3 eggs, beaten
⅔ cup milk
   Salt and pepper

Place bread cubes in a bowl; add beaten eggs, milk, and seasonings to taste (about 2 teaspoons salt and ¾ teaspoon pepper). Toss very lightly, as for a salad. Filling should be light, fluffy, slightly moistened, and well mixed, but not pressed together. Stuff turkey with about 4 cups of the filling. Generously salt and pepper the outside of the bird, truss, and place in roaster pan, breast down. Add 1 cup water and tent with heavy foil. Cook in a 375° oven for 4½ hours, removing foil and turning bird breast up for the last 30 minutes to brown the skin.

For gravy, remove and cut up giblets. Add 1 cup stock to pan juices, stirring with a wooden spoon to dissolve brown glaze on pan. Pour into a saucepan, stir in cornstarch and water paste (about 4 tablespoons cornstarch and ½ cup water), and cook, stirring, until smooth and thickened. Add cut-up giblets. Taste for seasoning.

While the turkey is cooking, bake the remaining filling. Generously butter a 1-quart baking dish and spoon in the filling, not packing it. Dot top lavishly with butter and bake in a 350° oven for 25 minutes, or until golden brown on top. Cover with foil and keep warm in turned-off oven until ready to serve.

Note: Bread Filling is great for stuffing pork chops (see p. 120) or beef heart, or just as a starchy vegetable instead of potatoes.

DRIED CORN IN CREAM

1 cup dried corn
2 cups milk
1½ teaspoons salt
2 teaspoons sugar
2 tablespoons butter
1 cup heavy cream

Soak the dried corn in the milk overnight in the refrigerator. Thirty minutes before serving time, put it in a pan with the remaining ingredients and bring to a boil. Reduce heat to low and simmer 30 minutes, stirring occasionally so it does not stick to the pan.

CRANBERRY SLUSH

1 pound fresh cranberries
½ cup water
1½ cups sugar
1 tablespoon lemon juice
2 cups grapefruit soda

Wash cranberries and put in a pan with the water. Bring to a boil. Cook until soft; then rub through a sieve. While the berries are still hot, add the sugar and lemon juice and stir until well blended. Cool; then add grapefruit soda and blend.

Pour into ice-cube trays or a cake pan and freeze until mushy. Serve with turkey, instead of a salad; the tartness makes a good contrast.

PUMPKIN CHIFFON PIE

1¼ cups strained cooked pumpkin
3 eggs, separated
1 cup brown sugar
1 tablespoon cornstarch
½ teaspoon salt
⅛ teaspoon ginger
⅛ teaspoon cloves
¼ teaspoon nutmeg
¾ teaspoon cinnamon
1¼ cups scalded milk
10-inch unbaked pie shell

Put pumpkin in a bowl. Beat in egg yolks, sugar, cornstarch, salt, and spices. Gradually beat in scalded milk, mixing thoroughly. Beat egg whites until stiff and fold into the mixture. Pour into pie shell and bake for 10 minutes at 400°; then reduce heat to 350° and continue baking for 40 minutes. Serve with whipped cream or ice cream.

Apple Pie Without Apples

Take 1 cup of sugar 1 teaspoonful tartaricacid 2 cups of water 1 cup of bread crumbed fine 1 egg, season with lemon or any thing you wish Let the water be warm when the bread is put in that it may soak

A winter feast at Groff's Farm.
Our paneled fireplace is a replica
of the one in the Pennsylvania Dutch room
at the Metropolitan Museum.

TWO WINTER SUPPERS

————————

FRIED SAUSAGE   RAW FRIED POTATOES   DILL PICKLES (PAGE 215)
CHOCOLATE PUDDING WITH APPLE SNOW
HOT MILK SPONGE CAKE WITH HOME-CANNED FRUIT

————————

So many people don't know what good country sausage is any more, but we are lucky. We always have plenty of fresh pork sausage or smoked sausage and it makes the best of all possible eating. Our sausage is made with nothing but ground pork, salt, and quite a lot of pepper, no other spices.

Raw fried potatoes with sliced raw onion on top are traditional in my family, and if you haven't tried this combination, you don't know what you're missing. We didn't use onion much in cooking, because Daddy always felt that a strong onion flavor could ruin a good dish.

The apple snow is something my mother makes to top tapioca or caramel pudding, or molded cranberry salad at Thanksgiving or Christmas. It's very low in calories and a great substitute for whipped cream if you are watching your weight. It could fool you; it looks like whipped cream. Apple snow should be made just before you serve the pudding, and it doesn't keep overnight. The hot milk sponge cake recipe comes from my good friend Kitty Brown, one of the best cooks I know.

RAW FRIED POTATOES

Wash and peel 2½ pounds of potatoes. Slice thinly and fry in 3 tablespoons shortening in a heavy skillet until golden brown, sprinkling with 2 teaspoons of salt. Turn often. When fried, cover with the lid and steam about 5 minutes. Serve with peeled raw onions, white or red, one for each two persons, to be sliced right on top of the potatoes.

CHOCOLATE PUDDING

4 tablespoons butter
3 cups milk
7 tablespoons cocoa
½ cup boiling water
1 cup granulated sugar
¼ cup cornstarch
¼ teaspoon salt
1 egg, beaten
1 teaspoon vanilla

Melt the butter. In a separate pan, warm the milk. Stir the cocoa and boiling water together to a paste; then mix in 3 tablespoons of the melted butter. Mix the sugar, cornstarch, and salt and mix into the milk. Add the cocoa-butter mixture, and the beaten egg. Cook over medium-low heat, stirring, until thick. Do not allow to boil. Remove from stove and mix in remaining 1 tablespoon melted butter and vanilla.

Cool. Serve topped with apple snow or whipped cream.

APPLE SNOW

2 egg whites
½ cup superfine sugar
½ apple, peeled and cored

Beat egg whites until fluffy; then gradually beat in sugar. Grate in the apple. Beat until mixture holds stiff peaks, like whipped cream.

HOT MILK SPONGE CAKE

4 eggs
1½ cups sugar
1½ cups flour
1 teaspoon baking powder
Pinch of salt
⅔ cup hot milk
1 heaping tablespoon butter
1 teaspoon vanilla

Cream the eggs and sugar. Sift together the flour, baking powder, and salt. Beat into the creamed mixture alternately with the hot milk, in which you have dissolved the butter, and the vanilla. Pour into a greased and floured 9 x 13-inch cake pan and bake in 350° oven for 45 minutes.

CREAMED SAUSAGE AND POTATOES   BUTTERED BEETS
LETTUCE WEDGES WITH SWEET AND SOUR DRESSING (PAGE 43)
BANANA CREAM PIE

Creamed sausage and potatoes, which is rather like scalloped potatoes, was a favorite family supper on cold winter nights. No matter how much was made, there was never any left over. With a vegetable or relishes and a salad, it makes a satisfying skillet dinner, a one-dish meal.

You can't believe how different beets taste when you grate them coarsely; they are just so buttery and delicious.

CREAMED SAUSAGE AND POTATOES

  2 pounds potatoes, peeled and very thinly sliced
  4 tablespoons flour
  1 teaspoon salt
 ⅛ teaspoon freshly ground pepper
  1 tablespoon chopped parsley or parsley flakes
1½ pounds sausage, cut in 1-inch cubes
  2 cups hot milk

Mix potatoes, flour, seasonings, and parsley until well blended. Fry sausage cubes in skillet until golden brown. Butter a 2-quart baking dish and put in a layer of half the potatoes; add half the sausage, then the rest of the potatoes and end with the rest of the sausage. Pour hot milk over them and bake in a 375° oven for 1 hour.

BUTTERED BEETS

2 pounds beets
1 teaspoon salt
2 tablespoons butter, melted

Wash beets, put in a pan with water to cover, and cook until soft. Peel and grate on a course grater. Sprinkle with salt and pour butter over them.

BANANA CREAM PIE

¾ cup sugar
3 tablespoons cornstarch
¼ teaspoon salt
2 cups milk
3 eggs, separated
1 tablespoon butter
1 tablespoon vanilla
1½ cups sliced bananas
9-inch baked pie shell
¼ teaspoon cream of tartar
4 tablespoons sugar

Combine the sugar, cornstarch, and salt and mix in 1½ cups of the milk. Cook in the top of a double boiler over hot water until thickened. Beat the egg yolks and add the remaining ½ cup milk. Add this egg mixture slowly to the custard and cook 2 minutes more. Remove from heat and mix in butter and vanilla. Cool.

Place sliced bananas in bottom of pie shell and cover with custard. Beat egg whites and cream of tartar to soft peaks; then beat in the 4 tablespoons sugar and continue beating until stiff and glossy. Cover custard with the meringue. Bake in 350° oven until meringue is golden brown, about 6 minutes.

A WINTER LUNCHEON

BETTY'S BEEF HASH   CAULIFLOWER WITH CHEESE SAUCE
MARINATED BEAN SALAD   WHITE MOUNTAIN CAKE

In my version of beef hash, the only leftover ingredient is beef; the vegetables are all fresh. The cauliflower with cheese sauce is something I serve a lot in the restaurant, and I found using white cheese gives it a much more delicate flavor. I can't claim that the bean salad is Pennsylvania Dutch; usually ours are just sweet-and-sour beans. This recipe was given to me by my friends Nancy and Jim McNiff, who came to Mount Joy from Michigan. I like it because it is colorful and the long marinating gives the canned beans lots of flavor. White Mountain cake is very traditional in Pennsylvania and a great favorite among the Amish, like chocolate cake. In fact, in a little book of recipes I have that was put together during the Depression by an Amishman, who typed it on a children's typewriter and sold it for a quarter, there are five White Mountain cakes and four chocolate cakes.

BETTY'S BEEF HASH

¼ cup shortening
4 cups diced roast beef
1 small onion, diced
2 cups sliced raw potatoes
2 green peppers, seeded and sliced
4 stalks celery, sliced
4 medium tomatoes, peeled, seeded, and sliced
  Salt, freshly ground pepper

Melt the shortening in a skillet and add the beef and onion. Brown lightly; then add the potatoes, peppers, celery, and tomatoes. Season to taste with salt and pepper. Cover with the lid and turn the mixture occasionally to prevent it burning, cooking until all the vegetables are soft.

CAULIFLOWER WITH CHEESE SAUCE

  1 firm head cauliflower
  1 cup water
1½ teaspoons salt
1½ teaspoons sugar
  2 tablespoons butter
  2 tablespoons flour
1½ cups milk or light cream
  ¼ pound grated white American cheese
  3 tablespoons Browned Butter (see p. 34)

Wash and trim the cauliflower. Boil 10 minutes in the water with the salt and sugar (either cook whole or break into flowerets to reduce the cooking time). Drain and keep hot while making sauce. Melt the butter in a saucepan, mix in the flour, and cook until golden and bubbling. Stir in the milk or cream, off the heat; then cook, stirring, until smooth and thickened. Add the cheese and stir until melted. Pour sauce over cauliflower and dribble the Browned Butter over the top.

MARINATED BEAN SALAD

  1 cup drained canned green beans
  1 cup drained canned yellow beans
  1 cup drained canned red kidney beans
  ½ cup green pepper, seeded and chopped
  1 small onion, chopped
  ¾ cup sugar
  ⅔ cup vinegar
  ⅓ cup salad oil
  1 teaspoon salt
  ½ teaspoon pepper

Combine the beans, pepper, and onion. Mix the sugar, vinegar, oil, salt, and pepper; pour over the beans and mix well. Marinate for 3 days in the refrigerator.

WHITE MOUNTAIN CAKE

⅔ cup shortening
1½ cups sugar
2½ cups cake flour
½ teaspoon salt
3½ teaspoons baking powder
¾ cup milk
1 teaspoon vanilla
4 egg whites
Caramel Icing (see p. 61)

Cream the shortening. Gradually add the sugar, creaming well until light and fluffy. Sift the flour, measure, add the salt and baking powder, and sift again. Add the dry ingredients to the creamed mixture alternately with the milk and flavoring, beating thoroughly after each addition. Beat the egg whites until stiff and fold into the mixture. Pour into two greased 9-inch layer cake pans. Bake in a 350° oven for 30 minutes. Cool and put layers together with Caramel Icing.

FIVE WINTER DINNERS

FRENCH TURKEY (FRESH BAKED HAM) (PAGE 53) WITH RAISIN SAUCE
FRIED SWEET POTATOES (PAGE 93)   WINE-GLAZED CARROTS
LIMA BEANS   SPICED WATERMELON RIND (PAGE 216)
CHOW CHOW (PAGE 220)   SHOOFLY CRUMB CAKE

There's nothing better than a plain baked, boiled, or fried sweet potato with pork or ham. Mother used to cook them with the skins on and freeze them whole; so we always had plenty on hand to fry.

The glazed carrot recipe is one I invented for the Christmas get-together of the Lancaster-York Wine Club, where everyone had to bring something made with wine. Very rarely do the women compliment you on your vegetables, but everyone wanted this recipe.

RAISIN SAUCE

½ cup brown sugar
1½ teaspoons prepared mustard
1 tablespoon flour
½ cup seedless raisins
½ cup red wine
1½ cups water

Mix the dry ingredients; then add the raisins, wine, and water. Bring to a boil; then simmer until syrupy.

WINE-GLAZED CARROTS

2 pounds scraped whole small carrots
1¼ teaspoons salt
½ cup butter
2 cups sugar
⅛ teaspoon nutmeg
¼ cup white wine

Cook carrots in water to cover with 1 teaspoon salt until tender, approximately 12 minutes. Drain and place in a shallow buttered baking dish.

Melt the butter in a heavy skillet and slowly stir in the sugar, remaining salt, and nutmeg. Stir with a wooden spoon until the sugar dissolves and turns a light caramel color. Stir in the wine and pour over the carrots. Heat in a 350° oven for 15 minutes.

SHOOFLY CRUMB CAKE

        4 cups flour
        1 cup granulated sugar
        1 cup light brown sugar
        1 teaspoon salt
        1 cup butter
        1 cup table molasses
        2 cups boiling water
     1¼ teaspoons baking soda

Mix the flour, granulated sugar, brown sugar, salt, and butter to crumbs, using a pastry blender or your fingers. Reserve 1 cup of the crumbs for topping.

Mix the molasses, boiling water, and baking soda and gradually add to the major part of the crumbs until well blended. Pour this mixture into a greased 9½ x 12¾-inch baking pan. Sprinkle the reserved 1 cup crumbs on top. Bake in a 350° oven for 55 minutes. (If you use layer-cake pans, decrease baking time to 40 minutes.)

This makes a very moist and unusual cake.

STUFFED PORK CHOPS
POTATOES BOILED IN THEIR JACKETS (PAGE 42)   TOMATO SAUCE
CREAMED COLE SLAW (PAGE 50)   CHOCOLATE-CHERRY SURPRISE

When we make tomato sauce, we thicken it with the brown flour paste, which gives it a lovely nutty rich flavor. Then try mashing the potatoes and pouring the sauce over them; that's good.

There's always plenty of leftover chocolate cake in our house, and this dessert is a neat way to use it up. I put my homemade cherry wine in it—that's the surprise—but you could use a sweet sherry, or a chocolate-flavored liqueur. For a spring party, I topped this with whipped cream, sank small straws in the cream, and put fresh purple violets in the straws; it was the prettiest thing you ever saw.

STUFFED PORK CHOPS

6 center pork chops, cut 1½ inches thick, with a pocket
  Bread Filling (see p. 104)
  Salt, freshly ground pepper
4 tablespoons butter

Stuff the chops with the Bread Filling and skewer the edges together with toothpicks to keep them closed. Season with salt and pepper. Melt the butter in a heavy skillet and cook the chops until golden brown on both sides, about 12 minutes. Place in a baking dish or pan and bake in a 350° oven for 30 minutes.

TOMATO SAUCE

4 tablespoons butter
½ cup flour
1 small onion, finely chopped
3 cups diced canned tomatoes
1 teaspoon salt
2 tablespoons brown sugar

Melt the butter in a heavy skillet and stir in the flour with a wooden spoon. Stir constantly over medium-low heat until golden brown, being sure it does not burn. Carefully mix in the remaining ingredients, blend well, and cook until thick.

CHOCOLATE-CHERRY SURPRISE

3 cups day-old chocolate cake crumbs
½ cup cherry wine (or sweet sherry or a liqueur)
3 cups vanilla ice cream
4 tablespoons milk
½ cup heavy cream, whipped
1 ounce dark sweet chocolate

Cover the bottom of a 1½-quart casserole dish with half the crumbs and dribble half the wine over them. Soften the ice cream with the milk, stirring until smooth. Put half the ice cream on top of crumbs. Cover with remaining crumbs, wine, and ice cream, in that order. Freeze until 20 minutes before serving time; then remove to refrigerator. Top with whipped cream and shave chocolate over the top.

HOME-CANNED BARTLETT PEARS (PAGE 212)
BAKED MEAT LOAF   WHOLE BROWNED POTATOES
BROCCOLI WITH BROWNED BUTTER (PAGE 34)
RAISIN PIE WITH ICE CREAM

Mother always said there's no point in canning a pear that isn't the best eating, and Bartletts are the finest. I like to leave the stems on, so when they are served it looks as if you just picked them.

Raisin pie is very traditional in our part of the country, probably because in the old days raisins were the one fruit you could have all year, but most raisin pies have a gummy texture and a pastry or crumb top that doesn't do much for them; so I made up my own recipe. Most people say they don't like raisin pie, but they like mine; it's more a raisin custard, not too sweet, and it is even better with whipped cream or ice cream.

BAKED MEAT LOAF

  2 pounds hamburger
  3 eggs, beaten
  1 tablespoon chopped parsley or parsley flakes
  1 cup drained canned tomatoes, chopped
  2 teaspoons salt
⅛ teaspoon pepper
  1 cup milk
  2 stalks celery, finely chopped
  2 cups fresh bread crumbs

Mix the meat with the eggs, parsley, tomatoes, seasonings, milk, celery, and bread crumbs, blending well. Form into 2 loaves, put in baking pan, and bake in a 375° oven for 1 hour and 15 minutes.

WHOLE BROWNED POTATOES

Scrub whole potatoes, one or two per serving, according to size. Boil in their skins in salted water until half-cooked. Drain, cool, and peel. Put the potatoes around the meat loaf and let them brown in the juices.

If you are frying ham, you can fry the potatoes in the ham fat after removing the ham from the skillet; then you get the extra golden brown color from the bits of ham that stick to the potatoes. Delicious served with the fried ham, green beans or beets, and warm rice pudding.

RAISIN PIE

    1 cup red wine
 1½ cups seedless raisins
    ¼ cup butter
    ¾ cup sugar
    3 eggs
    1 teaspoon vanilla
      9-inch unbaked pie shell

Heat the wine, add the raisins, and let them soak until plump.

Cream the butter and sugar. Beat in the eggs and vanilla (the mixture may look slightly curdled, but that doesn't matter). Add the raisins and wine, mix well, and pour into the pie shell. Bake in a 325° oven for about 50 minutes, or until filling is set. Cool before serving. Serve with ice cream or whipped cream.

FRIED HAM SLICES (PAGE 44)   POTATO CAKES
WARM RICE PUDDING WITH LEMON, CINNAMON, AND VANILLA
CANNED SOUR CHERRIES (PAGE 214)
OLD-FASHIONED CHOCOLATE CAKE WITH CARAMEL ICING
(PAGE 60)

We often serve rice pudding with ham, instead of as a dessert, and my slow method of cooking it makes it so smooth it just melts in your mouth. The canned sour cherries take the place of a relish or pickle; it's a good way to use them instead of in a pie. Some people would have what we call kippered cherries, which have been preserved in vinegar and sugar and left for a year.

POTATO CAKES

4 cups mashed potatoes
1 tablespoon chopped parsley
1 egg, slightly beaten
  Salt, freshly ground pepper to taste
  Flour

Mix the potatoes, parsley, egg, and seasonings (amount depends on how well the potatoes are seasoned). Pat into cakes
and roll in flour.

After frying the ham, remove it from the skillet and fry
the potato cakes in the ham fat until golden brown on both
sides. Garnish with sprigs of fresh parsley.

WARM RICE PUDDING WITH LEMON, CINNAMON, AND VANILLA

1 cup long grain rice
1 teaspoon salt
6 cups milk
¼ pound butter
4 tablespoons sugar
2 eggs, beaten

ADDITIONS

1 teaspoon vanilla, 1 tablespoon lemon juice, ¼ teaspoon cinnamon, or ¼ to ½ cup raisins, plumped in warm water

Boil the rice for 15 minutes in 2 cups water with ½ teaspoon
salt. Drain. Heat the milk, butter, and remaining salt in a
saucepan until butter melts. Add the rice and boil on very
low heat, lightly covered, for 1½ hours, stirring often to prevent sticking.

Remove from the heat and mix in the sugar and beaten

eggs. Reheat to just under a boil; do not allow it to boil. At this point, the pudding can be divided and flavored to individual taste with vanilla, lemon juice, cinnamon, raisins, or any desired combination of flavorings added.

CHICKEN AND DUMPLINGS   BUTTERED SPINACH (PAGE 85)
GREEN SALAD WITH OIL AND VINEGAR DRESSING
CHERRY CRUMB PIE

Chicken and dumplings—that's one of those old-fashioned recipes everyone tends to forget about, but nothing could taste better on a cold and wintry evening. The secret of having beautiful light dumplings, rather than heavy, doughy lumps, is to do them quickly and never, never to lift the lid from the minute you cover them to the time they are cooked.

That pinch of saffron in the cooking water makes all the difference to the chicken. We always put saffron to chicken in Lancaster County; it dates 'way, 'way back to the times when people had their own saffron beds. Why do thrifty farm folk use the world's most expensive spice so liberally? That's hard to say, but it is very traditional with us, and I think it may have been because of the Schwenkfelders, one of the religious groups from Germany which came to Pennsylvania in 1734. A Schwenkfelder family owned a saffron warehouse in Holland, and they must have brought some with them for the saffron-flavored yeast cake that was their wedding cake. I can even remember, when I was a child, seeing beds of the saffron crocus growing locally. One time I bought some bulbs and thought I'd give it a try, but something went wrong, and they never came up.

CHICKEN AND DUMPLINGS

        4-pound roasting chicken
    6 cups water
    2 teaspoons salt
    ⅛ teaspoon freshly ground pepper
        Pinch of saffron
    4 medium white potatoes, peeled and sliced thin
    1 small onion
    1 tablespoon chopped parsley
    4 medium stalks celery, coarsely chopped
1½ cups flour
    1 tablespoon baking powder
    1 teaspoon salt
    2 tablespoons butter
    1 egg
    ½ cup milk

Put the chicken in a Dutch oven or 5-quart casserole with the water, salt, pepper, and saffron. Bring to a boil, skim off the scum, reduce heat to a simmer, cover, and cook slowly until done, about 1 hour. Remove and cool chicken. When cool enough to handle, remove skin and bones and cut into chunks. Keep warm. Strain the broth and measure. You should have 6 cups. If not, add water.

Put the stock back in the pot, and add the vegetables and parsley. Cook for 15 minutes, before adding dumplings. Bring stock to a rapid boil.

To make dumplings, sift together the flour, baking powder, and salt. Cream the butter and egg together; then add the flour mixture and the milk alternately, beating well. Drop this mixture by tablespoons into the boiling liquid. When all are in, immediately cover the pot and boil, without removing the cover, for 12 minutes. Serve from the pot, with the pieces of chicken around the dumplings.

CHERRY CRUMB PIE

Follow recipe for Blueberry Crumb Pie (see p. 74), substituting 2½ cups pitted canned or frozen semisweet cherries for the berries, and omitting the nutmeg.

> ### Common gingerbread
>
> A pint of molasses half a pound of brown sugar 1 pound of fresh butter 2½ lbs of sifted flour A pint of milk A small teaspoonfull of pearlash.
>
> A tea cup full of ginger Cut the butter into the flour crush the sugar with a rooling pin and throw it into the flour and butter Add the ginger having dissolved the pearlash in the milk stir the milk and molasses alternately into the other ingrediants stir it very hard for a long time till it is quite light Put some flour on your past board take out small portions of the dough and make it with your hand into long rolls
>
> Then curl up the rolls into round cakes or twist 2 rolls together or lay them in straight lengths or sticks side by side and touching each other put them carefully in buttered pans and bake them in a moderate oven not hot enough to burn them if they should get scorched scrape off with a knife or grate all the burnt parts before you put the cakes away You can if you choose cut out the dough with tins the shape of hearts circles ovals or you may it all in one and cut it in squares when cold if the mixture appears to be too thin add gradually a little more sifted flour
>
> Elizabeth Miller 1845

Meet the family—
Abe, Betty, Johnny, Charlie,
and shaggy friend, Blackie the Labrador.

CHAPTER III

Food Makes Friends

WHEN WE STARTED serving dinners at the farm in 1961, it was to be my hobby, a means of my getting to meet more people, not a project that would involve the whole family, which is the way it has worked out. At the time, Abe was farming full-scale, with twelve acres of tobacco and a dairy herd, and I was helping him in the fields and around the farm.

My decision to cook for people was not based on any feeling that I was particularly knowledgeable or expert, but because my business experience had taught me that you should stick with what you know best. There was no question in my mind. I knew I had to serve the food that was part of my life and my background, the kind I cooked for my family.

I shall always remember Craig Claiborne, the Food Editor of the *New York Times,* telling me in 1965 that as long as I didn't change what I was doing one bit, I couldn't fail. A year later when Jim Beard came down to the farm he said the greatest contribution to food I could ever make would be to serve the kind of simple, home-style country dishes I had grown up with.

To have my own beliefs backed up by these two outstanding authorities in the food field really heartened me. My parents and aunts and friends—all the local people I felt were really good cooks—kept on saying, "Do you really think people will come from Philadelphia and New York to taste our kind of food?" To them it was an astonishment. To me it is no longer astonishing. I've found that is exactly what people *do* want to eat when they are here.

Our guests always comment that our food has such a different taste. What they really mean is that it is cooked with the best and freshest ingredients, and plenty of tender, loving care. I'm sure that is what makes our food a success—the quality and the simplicity. City people can have all the haute cuisine they want in their own restaurants. They like to come here because I cook in the old style and it brings back memories of the way food used to taste. The greatest compliment anyone can pay me is to tell me that eating at Groff's Farm is like eating at grandmother's house.

For the first five years, before Erma Engle came to assist me, I did all the cooking myself, and Abe helped with the carving and serving. I would bake the pies and cakes and get most of the food ready on the stove; then I'd tie a scarf around my head and go out to rake hay, or whatever had to be done.

Several times guests came early and caught me unawares. I'd get off the tractor, run over to them and say, "Just go in

Our guests are often surprised when I tell them I'm Mrs. Groff because they say I'm not the typical farmwife.

and make yourselves at home. Mrs. Groff will be there in a minute." Then I'd dash in the back door and upstairs, wash and change, and be down to greet them. We were always ready to serve right on time.

133

Frequently, people would ask to meet my mother, because they had it in their minds that I was going to be a little old farmwife, as wide as I was tall, wearing a bonnet and a print dress! Even now, someone is sure to stop me in the dining room and say, "Would it be possible to meet Mrs. Groff before we go home?" I tell them I think that can be arranged; then after dinner I come back and they see it really is me. Just because Abe and I dress like everyone else and wear clothes that are in style, it is hard for people to accept the fact that we are farmers. They expect the kind of stereotype they've seen on TV, the slow-witted, hay-chewing countryman. Today, farming is so highly mechanized and expensive that to run a successful operation you need some business ability and know-how, or you just aren't going to make ends meet. Like everybody else, we are getting more recreation-conscious, more aware that we need to take time off and get away from our routine. Abe is a good water-skier, and now he is taking up scuba diving with the boys; and we both love to travel. One of his hobbies is making reproduction furniture and one of mine is ceramics.

Running the restaurant is good for both of us. You need a quick wit and a sense of humor, because that is what turns people on and makes them feel at ease. Sometimes when I walk into the dining room the atmosphere is like ice, with everyone just sitting there and wondering what kind of place this is. They are so surprised to be greeted and talked to by a member of the family. We try to say a few words to all our guests, and both Charlie and Johnny love to serve in the dining room and meet people. In a way, you might say that the family has grown up with the business, because when we started Charlie was only three and Johnny wasn't even born. I would never have done anything to deprive my children. Instead, I think they have gained a much broader sense of the

Serving in the dining room is good experience for the boys.
Charlie is becoming an excellent waiter.

world and the people in it than most farm children ever get.

I remember in the very beginning, when one of the first bus groups was coming from Washington, I put up a map and showed Charlie where Washington, D.C. was. Then I told him about the Capitol and how the country was governed. From this early age he became interested in other parts of the country and looked forward to meeting the people. We'd make a game of it. As I baked pies or washed dishes I'd say, "I'm thinking of a big state," and he'd answer, "That must be Texas." Or I'd say, "I'm thinking of one that's known for potatoes," and he had it right off—Idaho. He'd jump off the kitchen chair, run over to the map, and point out the state.

One time a group of school teachers came from Norwich. Charlie was standing in the yard, petting his dog; he was only a little tyke. One of the teachers greeted him and asked his name. Then she said, "I'm sure you don't know where I live," and he told her he did, Connecticut. He went on to tell her the states and the ocean that bordered it and was she impressed.

It seemed there was always something funny happening. At first we used all our own furniture. It was very hard to keep those old Victorian chairs and sofas intact. One evening three large men sat on a little blue love seat only meant for two and of course it broke. We had it fixed, and I told Charlie, who was then about four, to sit in the room on his little stool when the guests were there and if he saw two people on the love seat to jump up and sit in the middle and talk to them. This worked all right for a few weeks until one afternoon he wasn't quite quick enough and suddenly realized there were three women on the love seat. He went over and said to them, "My mommy doesn't want three fat ladies to sit on that sofa."

Well, they thought that was hilarious, and just laughed and laughed, which really hurt Charlie's feelings. He came into the kitchen looking as if he was about to cry and told me he didn't know what he'd said, but it wasn't the right thing.

There were five of us living in the house then, including our adopted son, Bob Rote, who helped Abe with the farming. The guests liked to tour the house, because it is over 200 years old and has such an interesting construction; so we opened all the rooms—our room, the boys' and Bob's rooms, the guest room, even our own bathroom before we had separate toilets made in the upstairs hall. Between the first and second floors there is mudstraw cement for insulating and soundproofing, and Daddy cut a hole in the floorboards of Johnny's room so it could be seen. One evening I heard a lot of laughing upstairs and when I walked into the room I found that the children had been playing there and, hearing the guests coming, had thrown their toys—marbles, jacks, cards, all kind of junk —in the hole. When the board was lifted, there it all was. It did look funny, but I was a bit embarrassed.

Another time there was a big Christmas party and the women had piled their fur coats on Johnny's bed. When I came up to see if he was asleep, he was lying among the coats, his body curled to fit in between without touching them. After this, Abe and I decided we would cut out the upstairs tour and give the children back the privacy of their own rooms. I think it is sometimes hard for people to understand that the farm is our home, as well as a restaurant.

In those early days, we all worked like mules, but it was good, satisfying work, the kind you can do when you are young. By 1965 we had people coming from all over the world. One man from Portugal told me it was the first time he was ever in a restaurant where the owner went into the kitchen and made a fresh batch of pies when they ran out.

I'm often asked how people ever find out about Groff's Farm. We don't advertise, or have any signs or billboards in the vicinity. All our business is by reservation only. When we

Before Abe and I go out to seat the guests,
we make a last-minute check in the kitchen.

first started, the reservations came through The Willows restaurant. They took care of everything, including the checks.
The owners didn't want us to give out anything that showed
our name, address, or phone number; but they couldn't stop
people looking at the mailbox when they left.

During the first couple of years our neighbor, Ed Keene,
who was a mail carrier and sorter at the Mount Joy post office,
would find these letters addressed to "The Mennonite Cook in
Mount Joy," or "The Lady who serves Dinners in Mount
Joy" and pass them on to me.

Even though we have been in business since 1961, a lot
of the local people still don't know about us. Most of the
articles about Groff's Farm have appeared in out-of-town news-
papers and magazines, and people either hear of us this way
or by word of mouth. When they call or write for a reservation,
we give them instructions on how to get here, and though they
sometimes get lost, they always seem to find their way in
the end.

One man read about us in the *Christian Science Monitor*
while he was in Korea. When he came to visit his daughter,
who was a librarian at the War College in Carlisle, Pennsylvania, he asked her if she knew where this place in Mount Joy
might be. She didn't, but they decided to take a chance without reservations. They drove into Mount Joy and asked three
people to direct them to Groff's Farm. The first man said he
had lived in Mount Joy all his life and never heard of Groff's
Farm. The second man said he'd never heard of Groff's Farm
or the *Christian Science Monitor,* either. Finally, the third
man said he did know where it was, but he would never go
there. It was dreadfully expensive.

After dinner the man and his daughter told us their experiences and when we had finished laughing he said, "We
can't possibly eat dessert; we don't have room. We're going to

139

go back through Mount Joy, find that man who said you were so dreadfully expensive and tell him it's the best meal for the money we've ever had."

After the *Farm Journal* wrote about us, we had people driving hundreds of miles from the Midwest, just for dinner. As most of them didn't have reservations, we were turning away up to 200 a day. One Sunday I had just gotten up from an afternoon nap when the phone rang. The man at the other end asked if this was Groff's Farm. When I told him it was, he said, "Where the heck are you and what do you do there?" I told him we ran a restaurant on Pinkerton Road and enquired where he was from. Then he said, with quite a Dutch accent, "I'm from Main Street, Mount Joy, and every day I sit on my porch and these big cars pull up and they ask me where Groff's Farm is. I'm sure glad to know where you are and what's going on out there because I'll tell you, it makes me feel like an ass when I don't know what's happening in a town as small as this."

Now it seems that more and more of our guests are coming from other states and other countries. One night we took a roll call and there were people from Arizona, Michigan, Ohio, North Carolina, Australia, France, England, and Germany.

One of our very first experiences was with the International Beekeepers, who were meeting in Washington. Two bus loads came out two days in a row. There were at least eight or nine countries represented, with two interpreters. Everything was fine, the French were singing their songs and the Germans theirs, and everyone was running around taking pictures of the cows and the barns and the cornfields. The first day we served corn on the cob, not knowing that a lot of Europeans think corn is only for cattle. We showed them how to eat it, and they loved it. As they were leaving, one man came

Charlie and Cary Albright (nicknamed Tike)
are training for restaurant careers; so they pick up some tips
while giving Erma Engle a hand.

into the kitchen and quietly asked if I had any "maize" he could plant in his garden. I realized he meant corn, and fortunately I had about five pounds of seed corn left, so I put some in a plastic bag and gave it to him. When he got onto the bus, the others noticed it and came running in for corn. I gave away almost five pounds that day, and had to buy more. Next day's group wanted it, too. Everybody kidded me about using my seed corn to better international relations.

I noticed that two men in the second group, who I learned were Bulgarians, didn't seem at all happy. They couldn't understand the interpreters and didn't speak to anyone, just walked around talking to each other and taking notes and pictures.

When dinner was over, I got out my cornet and started to play for everyone to sing. One of the Bulgarians indicated that he'd like me to play a song for him. I gave him one of my favorites, "Open the Gates of the Temple." I played it with all my heart and soul and when I had finished, the Bulgarians came over to me with tears running down their cheeks. One of them fastened an honorary membership pin of a golden bee and a Bulgarian flag on me, and the other kissed my hand. If we couldn't get through in words, we sure got through with our music and our friendliness.

Since then we have had lots of international guests. They all seem to like our food, the Germans especially, because of course it is so similar to their own country cooking; and I think they enjoy sharing our way of life and being in the American countryside, which so few visitors have a chance to see.

I find that once people relax and feel at home with us, they really let go and enjoy themselves. If someone has a birthday, we sing and play "Happy Birthday," and Abe or I will give the woman or man a birthday kiss. After dinner, I bring

*Abe or I always stop by each table and visit a while,
to make the guests feel at home.*

When dinner is over, we say good-bye with music.

out my cornet, someone volunteers to play the piano and drums, and then things really start to swing. When it is time to go home, I break things up by playing "When the Saints Come Marching In" and lead everyone down to the wine cellar where they can have a sip of my homemade wine before leaving.

There is no better way to meet so many nice people being themselves. By the time we say good-bye, they are no longer customers, but friends.

DINNER AT GROFF'S FARM

CRACKER PUDDING (PAGE 94)
OLD-FASHIONED CHOCOLATE CAKE WITH CARAMEL ICING (PAGE 60)
FRESH FRUIT CUP *or* HAM AND BEAN SOUP
ROAST PRIME RIBS OF BEEF   BAKED COUNTRY HAM
CHICKEN STOLTZFUS
MASHED POTATOES WITH BROWNED BUTTER *or*
BREAD FILLING (PAGES 45, 34, AND 104)
HAPPY BEETS   GREEN BEANS IN HAM BROTH
PEPPER RELISH   CHOW CHOW   SPICED CANTALOUPE
SPICED WATERMELON RIND (PAGES 219, 220, AND 216)
SHOOFLY PIE *or* BLUEBERRY CRUMB PIE (PAGE 74)
or CHERRY CRUMB PIE (PAGE 129)
CHOICE OF   ICE CREAM   SHERBETS   CHOCOLATE SUNDAE

This is the basic restaurant menu, the one we started with, and the only change we made was to add a soup, because I found the guests expected one. We tried a couple of soups, but the favorite by far turned out to be the ham and bean soup, which really couldn't be simpler; it's the bits of home-cured baked ham that give it the flavor.

We always put cracker pudding and chocolate cake on the table before the appetizer is served, which surprises most people, but that's my way of doing things. I figure that your appetite is bigger at the beginning of a meal and, in case you don't have room later for dessert, you can have some right away.

The vegetables change according to the season and so do the pies (we always try to have two or three kinds of pies and ice cream), but the main course remains the same—roast beef, baked ham, and chicken Stoltzfus, a choice of two, or all three, according to the price of the dinner. The chicken Stoltzfus is probably the most popular of all our dishes; everyone wants it and they all ask where the name came from. Actually, it was one of those spur-of-the-moment things. This is our wedding chicken recipe and normally it would be served in patty shells, but it wouldn't have been possible to make shells for up to 150 people a night, which is our average—there wouldn't even have been a place to put them after they were baked—so I did it the way the Amish do, with little pastry squares. I can roll out, cut, and bake the squares in the morning when I'm making pie shells, ready to pop under the chicken.

When the Philadelphia *Bulletin* wrote up Groff's Farm, they wanted the name of the recipe and it didn't have one; so I just happened to think of our dear Amish friends, Elam and Hannah Stoltzfus, and that's what it became.

The happy beets are another story—rather a funny one. They are what got me into the business of winemaking. We Mennonites aren't a drinking people, but we did make wine for mincemeat. When I got married and needed wine for my mince pies, rather than go to the state liquor store and buy some I did what the farm people in our neighborhood do. I took some of the juice from the home-canned fruits, put it in jugs with sugar, added a couple of drops of water each day as it began to ferment and foam over, and when it cleared, there was my first wine, a beautiful syrupy red wine from cherry and damson plum juice. From then on, I always had a jug or two of wine down cellar for the mince pies.

About five years after we started the restaurant I hired my neighbor lady, Erma Engle, to help me cook, so she could take over when I went to change and meet my guests. I couldn't work hard all day if I couldn't enjoy my guests in the evening.

I noticed Erma was having trouble with the Harvard beet sauce, and she told me she'd had the worst time finding any vinegar, we seemed to be out of it, and now her sauce didn't taste at all like mine, though she'd done exactly what I told her. I took a taste and it was delicious, much better than mine; all it needed was a little salt and sugar. I asked her where she had found the vinegar and when she said, " 'Way back in the far corner of the cellar," I broke up, because that wasn't vinegar, that was the wine for my mince pies. Everyone raved about the beets that night; so we never did go back to the old Harvard beet recipe and I told Erma that was the nicest mistake she ever made. We dubbed them our "happy beets" and we tell people, "If you don't like beets, drink the sauce."

When I started the restaurant I knew everyone would expect me to serve shoofly pie (it's such a local specialty), but no one in my family was fond of it. I had just three weeks to find a recipe that suited me; that's when the first dinner group was coming from Washington. For two weeks straight I baked a different shoofly pie every day from someone's recipe, and it got so I could almost tell by looking at the recipe whether it would be any good or not. Finally, I combined two recipes, half of one, half of the other, put the pie on the table, and asked Abe what he thought of it. He said, "It's good—great just the way it is," and then "Have you forgotten how to make any other kind of pie?"

I've never been quite sure whether he really liked it or was just so tired of eating shoofly pie he'd decided this had to be it, the last one; but the minute we started serving it the guests said they'd never had a shoofly pie like ours and so we were almost forced to make it. Fortunately, this is the one pie you can freeze. If you make a whole batch and freeze what you don't use, you can reheat them slightly, just bring them to a warm, and the goo is just as gooey and the cake part just as fresh. This isn't a pie to eat if you are watching calories, but it's part of being in the Pennsylvania Dutch area and the guests want to try it; it's something that sticks in their memories.

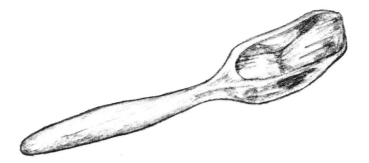

HAM AND BEAN SOUP

    2 cups milk
    2 cups canned Great Northern beans
    1 cup chopped baked country-cured ham
    ½ teaspoon coarsely ground black pepper
    1 tablespoon chopped parsley

The canned beans are better for this soup than the dried ones you cook yourself; they hold up better and don't get mushy.

Heat the milk, stir in the beans, ham, pepper, and parsley and simmer 20 minutes.

The usual kitchen scene:
Erma debones chicken for chicken Stoltzfus
while waitress Marian Conner snatches a bite
before the rush starts.

CHICKEN STOLTZFUS

    5-pound roasting chicken, cut into 8 pieces
4 quarts water
1 tablespoon salt
6 black peppercorns
¼ teaspoon ground saffron
12 tablespoons butter
12 tablespoons (¾ cup) flour
2 cups light cream
¼ cup finely chopped parsley
    Pastry Squares (see below)

When I make Chicken Stoltzfus, I use a large roasting chicken; it has much more fat and flavor.

Put the chicken in an 8-quart pan with the water, and bring to a boil. Skim off the scum; then add the salt, peppercorns, and saffron. Reduce heat, partially cover, and simmer for 1 hour. Remove chicken and cool a little. Strain stock and reserve 6 cups. When chicken is cool enough to handle, remove skin and bones and cut meat in bite-size pieces.

Melt the butter and mix in the flour. Cook over medium-low heat until golden and bubbling; then stir in the reserved chicken stock and the cream, stirring constantly, and cook over high heat until the sauce comes to a boil. Simmer until thickened and smooth. Reduce heat, add chicken pieces and parsley.

While chicken is simmering, make the pastry squares.

PASTRY SQUARES

⅔ cup lard
⅓ cup butter
3 cups all-purpose flour
1 teaspoon salt
½ cup (approximately) ice water

Cut the lard and butter into the flour and salt with a pastry blender, or mix with your fingers until it forms crumbs. Sprinkle ice water over crumbs with left hand while tossing crumbs lightly with right hand, using only enough water to keep the dough together. Press dough into a ball and place on a lightly floured surface. Divide in 2 parts. Roll out each part in a large rectangle on ungreased cooky sheets (roll the dough directly onto the sheets), about ⅛ inch thick. Cut dough into 1-inch squares with a pastry wheel or sharp knife.

Bake in a 350° oven for 12 to 15 minutes, until lightly browned.

Arrange the pastry squares on a platter and spoon the chicken mixture over them.

HAPPY BEETS

    4 cups Pickled Beets (see p. 220)
    4 cups beet juice from jars
    ½ cup tart homemade wine, such as rhubarb or dry red wine
    2 tablespoons arrowroot, dissolved in ¼ cup water

Heat beet juice; then stir in the wine and dissolved arrowroot. Cook, stirring, until thickened. Add beets and cook 2 minutes. Taste and adjust seasoning, adding salt and sugar as required.

Note: The tarter the wine, the better the beets.

GREEN BEANS IN HAM BROTH

    2 pounds green beans
    1 cup ham broth (see p. 54)
    ½ cup water
        Salt, freshly ground pepper

Wash and trim the beans. Bring broth and water to a boil in a saucepan; add beans and salt and pepper to taste (the amount of salt depends on the saltiness of the ham broth). Boil approximately 12 minutes; do not overcook. Serve in the liquid.

SHOOFLY PIE

CRUMB TOPPING

1 cup unsifted flour
½ cup light brown sugar
¼ cup vegetable shortening

LIQUID BOTTOM

1 teaspoon baking soda
1 cup boiling water
1 cup golden table molasses
¼ teaspoon salt
  9-inch unbaked pie shell

Combine the flour, brown sugar, and shortening in a bowl and cut with a pastry blender or rub with your fingers until it forms fine crumbs.

Dissolve the soda in the boiling water in a bowl; add the molasses and salt and stir to blend well. Pour liquid mixture into the unbaked pie shell and sprinkle the crumb topping evenly over it. Bake in a 375° oven for 10 minutes; then reduce the temperature to 350° and bake for 30 minutes longer, or until set (when the pie is given a gentle shake, the top should remain firm). Serve warm with whipped cream or ice cream.

CHOCOLATE SYRUP

This chocolate syrup is nice to make ahead and keep in the refrigerator for chocolate sundaes or shakes. It will last for a long time. The recipe came from a little ice cream shop in the county that was known for its chocolate syrup. They were nice enough to let me have it for the restaurant.

    2 cups Hershey's cocoa
    8 cups (4 pounds) sugar
    1 teaspoon salt
    3 quarts water
    2 tablespoons arrowroot, dissolved in ¼ cup water
    1 tablespoon vanilla

Sift the cocoa, sugar, and salt. Put in a 5-quart pan and gradually whisk in the water over medium heat. Bring to a boil, stirring constantly. As it comes to the boil, mix in the arrowroot and cook for 5 minutes, until thickened. Remove from heat and stir in the vanilla. This makes a good 3 quarts or more of syrup.

———

Our Colonial Night dinners started in 1972 and they came about because I was writing a food column for a bicentennial paper, which meant going back into the old cookbooks and recipes of our area, researching and testing them. As I was testing them, I'd invite six people to dinner so I could do a whole menu at one time. Then the local people who came to the restaurant began saying, "Can I come back and have those croquettes?" or whatever it was I'd served; so I decided that one night a week I would do a special menu for a limited number of people. Tuesday, Friday, and Saturday are our busiest nights, Tuesday and Friday being market days, and Saturday the weekend. Wednesday was always one of the slower evenings; so that was the night I picked. Now it has become so popular that the local people come just to see what's going on. Wednesday has become Betty's surprise night, the night I can do whatever I feel like and use all the fresh seasonal foods, like new scraped potatoes, that you can't begin to prepare for a big group.

*With Erma Engle and John Boyer, the kitchen runs smoothly
no matter how busy we are. John, who works as a butcher in a supermarket,
comes in to carve on weekends, or nights
when we have a lot of reservations.*

*Erma, my good right hand, does everything from cooking to serving.
Here she ladles out bean soup
for one of the waitresses, Mary Stahl.*

CREAM OF WATERCRESS SOUP
CHICKEN AND MUSHROOMS IN PATTY SHELLS (PAGE 98)
SCALLOPED OYSTERS   RICED POTATOES
PEPPERS STUFFED WITH CHEESE   LEMON SPONGE PIE

I found the watercress soup in an 1850 cookbook. The recipe called for veal stock, but I prefer to use chicken, of which I always have lots on hand. Watercress grows wild in the streams around our place, so this soup was a natural for me.

The scalloped oysters are my version of my mother's recipe; I'm more liberal with the cream and make it a bit richer.

Plain old boiled potatoes taste and look much more elegant if you put them through a food press and just let them fall into a mound in the dish. They come out looking light and fluffy, like rice.

CREAM OF WATERCRESS SOUP

  3 cups rich, well-seasoned chicken stock
  2 cups coarsely chopped watercress
  4 tablespoons butter
⅓ cup flour
  1 cup light cream
    Green food coloring (optional)

GARNISH: *Watercress sprigs, seasoned croutons*

Put the stock in a pan, add the watercress, and simmer 12 minutes to extract the flavor. Strain and reserve the stock.

Melt the butter, stir in the flour, and cook until golden and bubbling. Slowly add the stock, stirring constantly, and cook until thickened. Add the cream and heat through. Tint this with a few drops of green food coloring, if you like, to give it a watercress color. Serve garnished with a sprig of watercress and a few seasoned croutons in each cup or plate.

SCALLOPED OYSTERS

    3 dozen medium oysters (2½ cups) with their liquor
    1 cup fresh bread crumbs
    ½ teaspoon salt
      Freshly ground pepper
    ½ cup melted butter
    2 cups small oyster crackers
    1 cup heavy cream

Check the oysters for tiny bits of shell. Line a buttered 1½-quart casserole with ¼ cup bread crumbs. Add half the oysters and sprinkle with salt and pepper. Add ½ cup bread crumbs, ¼ cup butter, the oyster crackers, cream, and liquor from oysters. Add remaining oysters; sprinkle with remaining bread crumbs and butter. Bake in a 375° oven for 35 minutes.

RICED POTATOES

Peel 2 pounds white potatoes and cook in salted water until soft. Drain and dry over low heat. Put potatoes through ricer or food press so they fall into the serving dish in a fluffy mound. Pour 4 tablespoons Browned Butter (see p. 34) over the top.

PEPPERS STUFFED WITH CHEESE

6 large green bell peppers
1 tablespoon chopped onion
5 tablespoons butter
2 cups bread crumbs
3 cups grated white American cheese
½ teaspoon salt
⅛ teaspoon freshly ground pepper

Slice off the stem end of the peppers and remove the seeds and ribs. Parboil in boiling water for 5 minutes and drain, upside down, on paper towels.

Fry the onion in 1 tablespoon butter until just soft. Combine with the bread crumbs, 2 cups cheese, remaining butter, and seasonings, mixing well. Fill peppers with this mixture and sprinkle the remaining cheese on the top. Put in a greased baking dish and bake in a 375° oven for 30 minutes.

LEMON SPONGE PIE

2 tablespoons vegetable shortening
1 cup sugar
½ teaspoon salt
3 tablespoons flour
2 large or 3 small eggs, separated
1 cup milk
¼ cup lemon juice
1 tablespoon grated lemon rind
9-inch unbaked pie shell

Cream the shortening, sugar, and salt until light and fluffy. Beat in the flour. Beat the egg yolks and mix with the milk and lemon juice. Add to the creamed mixture with the lemon rind. Beat egg whites until stiff and fold in. Pour into the pie shell and bake in a 375° oven for about 10 minutes; then reduce heat to 350° and continue baking for 35 minutes.

FRIED OYSTERS (PAGE 97)   ROAST DUCK WITH APPLE STUFFING
BRUSSELS SPROUTS WITH CHESTNUTS   MASHED POTATOES (PAGE 45)
BAKED CORN PUDDING   FRENCH CAKE

The roast duck with apple stuffing and the Brussels sprouts with chestnuts are recipes I found while doing research for my bicentennial column. This is a lovely stuffing, delicate yet crunchy. Brussels sprouts and chestnuts were apparently a very popular combination in the mid-1800s for dinner parties. I had friends in on the evening I tried this dish. One man detested Brussels sprouts; but after he'd taken just one mouthful he said, "Those chestnuts sure do a lot for Brussels sprouts." And so they do.

ROAST DUCK WITH APPLE STUFFING

   5-to-6-pound duck
   Salt
  6 slices bacon
 ½ cup chopped celery
 ¼ cup chopped onion
 ¼ cup chopped parsley
 ½ cup sugar
 4 cups peeled, cored, and diced apples
 1 cup cracker crumbs
   Freshly ground pepper

Rinse and clean the duck and sprinkle the inside lightly with salt. Fry bacon and drain on paper towels. Break into bits. Sauté the celery, onion, and parsley in the bacon fat for 10 minutes on low heat. Remove and place in a large mixing bowl.

Add the sugar to the remaining fat in the pan; add the apples and sauté, shaking the pan, until the apples are golden and almost soft. Put apples, bacon bits, and cracker crumbs in the mixing bowl with the vegetables and toss together until well blended.

Fill the duck with the apple stuffing, about ⅔ full. With skewers and cord, close the openings. Truss the bird and season the outside with salt and pepper. Put in a covered roasting pan and cook in a 400° oven for 4 hours, uncovering for the last 30 minutes to brown the skin.

Remove duck, skim fat from pan juices, add 3 cups water, and simmer until all the brownings are dissolved. Thicken with ¼ cup arrowroot or cornstarch dissolved in ¼ cup water. Season to taste and, if desired, add the giblets from the duck, simmered in seasoned water, or baked until done, and chopped finely.

There will probably be too much stuffing for the bird.

Place whatever is left over in a buttered casserole, dot the top with a little butter, and bake in a 350° oven for 30 minutes.

BRUSSELS SPROUTS WITH CHESTNUTS

    1 quart Brussels sprouts, cleaned and trimmed
    2 cups water
      Salt
    7 tablespoons butter
    1 cup boiled or canned chestnuts
    1 tablespoon sugar
  1/3 cup beef stock
      Freshly ground pepper

Cook the sprouts in 2 cups water and 1 teaspoon salt until just tender, but still firm. Drain. Melt 3 tablespoons butter in a heavy skillet, add the sprouts, and sauté until just lightly colored.

If you are using fresh chestnuts, cut a gash on one side of the nut, put them in a pan with water to cover and 1 teaspoon salt, and cook for 15 minutes. Drain, and when just cool enough to handle, remove shell and skin.

Melt 4 tablespoons butter in a skillet and add the sugar. Cook, stirring, until brown and lightly caramelized. Add chestnuts and cook until golden brown. Add beef stock, 1/2 teaspoon salt, and 1/8 teaspoon pepper. Pour this over the Brussels sprouts and simmer a few minutes.

BAKED CORN PUDDING

2½ cups fresh or frozen corn, cut off the cob
1 tablespoon sugar
1 teaspoon salt
⅛ teaspoon freshly ground pepper
1½ tablespoons flour
2½ tablespoons melted butter
3 eggs, beaten
1 cup milk

If the corn is frozen, let it thaw. Combine corn with remaining ingredients and pour into a 1½-quart baking dish. Bake in a 350° oven for 35 minutes. (This can be baked in the same oven as the stuffing.)

FRENCH CAKE

½ cup butter
2 cups granulated sugar
3 eggs
3 cups sifted flour
4 teaspoons baking powder
½ teaspoon salt
1 cup milk
1 teaspoon vanilla
Caramel Icing (see p. 61)

Cream the butter and sugar until light and fluffy. Add the eggs, one at a time, beating well after each addition. Sift together the flour, baking powder, and salt. Add to the creamed mixture alternately with the milk; then add the vanilla. Pour into 3 greased and floured 8-inch layer cake pans and bake in a 350° oven for approximately 35 minutes. When cool, put layers together and ice top with Caramel Icing.

DEVILED CLAMS   ROAST CHICKEN WITH CHESTNUT STUFFING
FRIED APPLE RINGS   BUTTERED CARROTS   WILTED SALAD
CHERRY CRUMB PIE (PAGE 129) WITH ICE CREAM

The first experience I ever had with deviled clams was at a family dinner Abe's grandmother had for us when we were first married—and I loved them. I've loved them ever since. Her recipe, which came from her mother, uses beaten eggs and the clams are fried. Erma Engle's recipe is a little bit different; so I'm including both versions.

I found the chestnut filling in an old cookbook when I was doing my Colonial recipe research; chestnuts were very popular in the old days, before we got the blight on the chestnuts in this country, and this stuffing is so rich and good you can't stop eating it.

ERMA ENGLE'S DEVILED CLAMS

10 large clams
4 hard-boiled eggs
½ medium onion
2 large ribs celery
½ large green pepper
2 tablespoons chopped parsley
4 cups fresh bread crumbs
Salt, freshly ground pepper
1 tablespoon butter

Chop the clams into small pieces. Mince the eggs coarsely. Chop the onion, celery, and pepper very finely (a blender does a good job of this). Mix the clams, eggs, vegetables, parsley, and bread crumbs until well blended. Season to taste with salt and pepper. Scrub 10 clam shells and butter the insides. Fill with the clam mixture and arrange on a cooky sheet. Bake in a 375° oven until golden brown, about 25 minutes. Serve 2 clams per person.

MRS. BOMBERGER'S DEVILED CLAMS

Use 4 beaten eggs instead of the hard-boiled eggs in the preceding recipe. After filling the shells, fry the clams upside down in hot butter or oil until golden brown.

ROAST CHICKEN WITH CHESTNUT STUFFING

6-pound roasting chicken
Salt, freshly ground pepper
3 cups boiled chestnuts or canned chestnuts
½ cup melted butter
¼ cup light cream
½ cup cracker crumbs (saltines)

Clean chicken and rub the inside with salt. Chop the chestnuts (this can be done in the blender). Add the butter, cream, and cracker crumbs and salt and pepper to taste. Mix well. Stuff the chicken, close the openings with skewer and cord, truss, and rub the skin well with salt and pepper. Place in a roaster, cover, and cook in 375° oven for 3½ hours. Uncover for the last 15 minutes to brown the skin. Remove chicken to a hot platter and keep warm.

Skim the fat from the pan juices, add 3 cups water, and simmer to dissolve the browning. Thicken gravy with cornstarch and water paste, and serve with the chicken and stuffing.

FRIED APPLE RINGS

3 large firm apples, such as Delicious
3 tablespoons butter
1 tablespoon sugar

Core the apples, but leave the skin on. Slice in rings ¼ inch thick. Melt butter in a heavy skillet, add the apple slices, and sprinkle with the sugar. Fry on medium heat until golden brown; turn and fry on the other side.

BUTTERED CARROTS

    1 pound carrots
    1 cup water
1½ teaspoons salt
1½ teaspoons sugar
    2 tablespoons Browned Butter (see p. 34)

Scrub carrots and cut in ¼-inch-thick slices. Put in a saucepan with the water, salt, and sugar and bring to a boil. Boil just until tender, about 12 minutes. Drain, put in a serving dish, and pour the Browned Butter over them.

WILTED SALAD

Follow directions for Dandelion Salad with Hot Bacon Dressing (see p. 35), substituting other salad greens of your choice (bitter greens are best with this dressing).

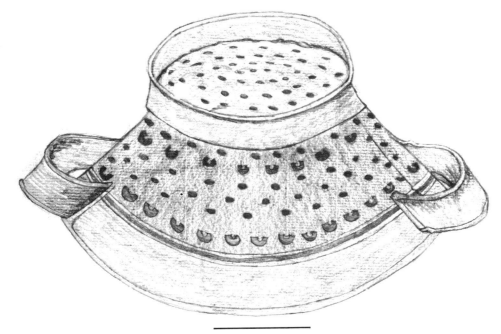

SPLIT PEA SOUP   ROAST PORK LOIN (PAGE 53)
SCALLOPED POTATOES   JACKIE'S BAKED CABBAGE
PICKLED BEETS (PAGE 220)   BAKED APPLE CRISP WITH ICE CREAM

Everyone in the restaurant asks for our scalloped potato recipe; the trick is in grating the potatoes instead of slicing them, and you have to do them quickly and get them into the flour and milk before they turn pink.

Even my father, who doesn't like cabbage, said he could make a whole meal from Jackie's baked cabbage. Jackie Mc-Guigan is my neighbor; she lives on Pinkerton Road, right across the street from Erma Engle. It seems like Pinkerton Road is full of good cooks. Incidentally, here's an old-fashioned tip for killing the odor of boiling cabbage: put a small pan of water on the stove, let it steam, then add ½ teaspoon powdered cinnamon and ½ teaspoon powdered cloves. It smells much pleasanter than those air-deodorizing sprays.

SPLIT PEA SOUP

1 pound dried split peas
3 quarts water
1 teaspoon salt
1 onion
1 small rib celery
   1-pound piece of home-cured ham
2 cups milk
   Dash of pepper

Clean and wash the peas. Put in a pan with the water, salt, onion, celery, and ham and cook slowly for 3 hours. Remove the celery, onion, and ham. Put peas and liquid in a blender and blend until smooth. Heat the milk and add the pureed peas. Season with pepper to taste.

SCALLOPED POTATOES

2½ pounds white potatoes
 6 tablespoons flour
2½ teaspoons salt
 ⅛ teaspoon freshly ground pepper
 3 tablespoons butter
 2 cups milk

Peel and grate the raw potatoes, using a grater or salad maker, and immediately add to the flour, salt, and pepper, stirring with a wooden spoon until thoroughly mixed. Put half the potato mixture in a 2-quart buttered baking dish, dot with 1 tablespoon of the butter, add the remaining potatoes, and dot with the remaining 2 tablespoons butter. Pour milk over the potatoes and bake in a 350° oven for 1¼ hours. If the potatoes are not golden brown on the top, put under the broiler for a couple of minutes.

JACKIE'S BAKED CABBAGE

  1 medium head cabbage
  2 tablespoons flour
  1 teaspoon salt
 ⅛ teaspoon freshly ground pepper
  2 tablespoons sugar
  3 tablespoons butter
  1 cup hot milk
 ½ cup grated cheese

Cut cabbage in wedges ¼-inch thick. Boil in water for 10 minutes. Drain well and place in a buttered casserole. Sprinkle with the flour, salt, pepper, and sugar. Dot with butter. Pour the hot milk over the cabbage and top with the grated cheese. Bake in a 350° oven for 35 minutes.

BAKED APPLE CRISP

  5 cups peeled, cored, and sliced baking apples
 ½ cup water
  1 cup flour
  1 cup light brown sugar
 ½ cup butter
 ½ teaspoon cinnamon
 ½ teaspoon salt

Place apples in a buttered 1½-quart baking dish. Add water. Combine the flour, sugar, butter, cinnamon, and salt, rubbing with your fingers until it forms fine crumbs. Spread the crumbs over the apples. Bake in a 375° oven for about 40 minutes, uncovered. Serve cold, topped with whipped cream, or warm, with ice cream.

FRESH FRUIT CUP *or* CHICKEN-RICE SOUP
WEINER SCHNITZEL   PARSLEYED POTATOES
TOMATO SAUCE WITH CROUTONS AND HARD-BOILED EGGS
SALAD OF LETTUCE AND SPINACH *or*
WATERCRESS, SWEET AND SOUR DRESSING (PAGE 43)
RYE BREAD AND BUTTER
CORNSTARCH PUDDING WITH FRESH FRUIT
or HOME-CANNED BERRIES

To make a good chicken-rice soup, it's the quality of the chicken that counts, and the heavier the chicken, the better. I never use anything under a 4-pound chicken, usually a 6-pound roaster.

Although we didn't use a lot of veal in our area—the heifers and the vealers were raised for market—we do like weiner schnitzel. We prefer veal cooked that way because we are great for frying things. My grandfather, at ninety, felt he knew better than we when he'd had enough fried oysters and he ate eight before we got him stopped.

The tomato sauce with buttered croutons is something we do a lot in the restaurant, and this recipe is a combination of my family's way of doing it and Erma's. She uses onion and we didn't, we put toasted buttered crumbs or croutons on top, and she likes slices of hard-boiled egg. There must be something universal about this dish, because I've had a lot of people kid me and say they had grandma's tomatoes today.

CHICKEN-RICE SOUP

    6 cups rich, well-seasoned stock
    ½ cup finely chopped celery
    1 tablespoon chopped parsley
    1 cup cooked rice
    1½ cups diced cooked chicken

Bring the stock to a boil and add the celery, parsley, and rice. Boil 10 minutes. Add the chicken and just heat through before serving.

WEINER SCHNITZEL

    2 pounds veal scallops, cut from leg, sliced ¼ inch thick
      Flour
      Butter for frying
      Salt, freshly ground pepper

Flour the veal by putting the flour in a flat dinner plate and patting both sides of the veal into the flour.

Melt the butter in a heavy skillet and add the veal. Lightly salt and pepper one side and fry until golden brown on both sides; this should take only a few minutes. Fry only as many pieces of veal at one time as you can get in the pan without crowding.

TOMATO SAUCE WITH CROUTONS AND HARD-BOILED EGGS

4 cups canned, diced tomatoes, with juice
1 teaspoon salt
2 tablespoons brown sugar
½ medium onion, chopped finely
   A little freshly ground pepper
3 tablespoons arrowroot dissolved to a paste in ¼ cup water
½ cup buttered croutons
1 hard-boiled egg, sliced

Drain the tomatoes. Put the juice in a pan with the salt, sugar, onion, and pepper. Bring to a boil and simmer just long enough to cook the onion. Add the arrowroot paste and cook, stirring, until thickened. Add the tomatoes and heat through. Garnish the sauce with the croutons and egg slices. I like to make my croutons by baking bread cubes in the oven with plenty of butter for 3 or 4 hours, until they get crisp, brown, and really rich.

CORNSTARCH PUDDING

1 quart and ¼ cup milk
⅔ cup sugar
5 tablespoons cornstarch
¼ teaspoon salt
2 eggs, beaten
1 teaspoon vanilla

Scald the 1 quart milk in a double boiler. Combine the sugar, cornstarch, salt, beaten eggs, and ¼ cup milk. Add to the scalded milk and cook, stirring, until thickened, about 4 minutes. Remove from heat and add vanilla. Cool and serve garnished with fruit.

TOMATO JUICE SEASONED WITH TABASCO, LEMON JUICE,
AND PEPPER (PAGE 222)
ROAST PORK LOIN (PAGE 53)   BAKED ONIONS
SAUERKRAUT IN BEER   MASHED POTATOES (PAGE 45)
APPLESAUCE (PAGE 51)   CARAMEL PUDDING

Nothing is better with pork than sauerkraut—and when you cook it in beer, it is much easier to digest. The whole baked onions are unbelievably delicious and so sweet; you just cut them open and put a pat of butter on them.

Caramel pudding was one of my husband's favorite puddings, but it took me seven years to find out! Every year we went to his home for Thanksgiving, and Abe's mother made all the things her nine children used to like and never once mentioned it. Now I quite often make it on Wednesday nights because once anyone has tasted it, they love it, too. It's very rich, smooth, and creamy. When you add the brown sugar and salt you actually almost let it burn. It should really caramelize before you add the milk; so you have to be very careful. This also makes a great pie, with whipped cream.

BAKED ONIONS

Peel 6 medium-sized white onions and place in a baking dish. Bake in a 350° oven for 50 to 60 minutes. Sprinkle with salt before serving. They should be cut in half when served and a pat of butter put on them.

SAUERKRAUT IN BEER

Wash and drain 2 pounds sauerkraut and put in a pan. Cover with beer and simmer 20 minutes.

CARAMEL PUDDING

 2 tablespoons butter
 1 cup light brown sugar
 ½ teaspoon salt
 3 cups milk
 1 tablespoon flour
 2½ tablespoons cornstarch
 2 eggs, beaten
 1 teaspoon vanilla

Melt the butter in a heavy skillet. Add the brown sugar and salt and cook, stirring well, until sugar caramelizes. Slowly mix in 2 cups milk and heat to boiling point, stirring constantly with a wire whip or wooden spoon. Mix the remaining milk, flour, and cornstarch to a paste. Add to mixture, stirring constantly, and cook until thickened. Add 1 cup of the hot mixture to the eggs, beat, and then add to the pudding. Cook 2 minutes, but do not let the pudding boil. Remove from heat and add the vanilla. Serve warm, or chilled with whipped cream.

POTATO SOUP   GOLDEN GEMS OF LAMB
HOMEMADE NOODLES (PAGE 39)
BROCCOLI WITH BROWNED BUTTER (PAGE 34)
CUCUMBER, ONION, AND TOMATO SALAD   RAISIN PIE (PAGE 124)

When I was first married, I never found a potato soup that did anything for me; so I made up my own recipe. It's a country-style potato soup, the kind that is almost a meal in itself; so the main course should be something light.

The golden gems of lamb is another old recipe I unearthed in my research and it is rather unusual; the directions in the nineteenth-century cookbook told you how to trim the meat from the leg and called it the filet. I suppose that in those days the marinade helped to disguise the strong flavor of meat that may not have been quite fresh, but it does give lamb a delicacy and a delicious taste.

POTATO SOUP

  4 cups diced white potatoes
½ cup chopped celery
¼ cup chopped onion
¼ cup chopped parsley
  4 cups water
  1 teaspoon salt
½ teaspoon celery salt
⅛ teaspoon freshly ground pepper
  2 cups light cream
  4 hard-boiled eggs, sliced
  3 tablespoons butter
    Sprigs of fresh parsley

Combine the vegetables, water, and seasonings in a pan and

boil until vegetables are tender, not mushy. Add the cream and sliced hard-boiled eggs and bring to just under the boiling point. Add the butter. Serve garnished with parsley.

GOLDEN GEMS OF LAMB

2 pounds lamb from the leg, cut in 1-inch-wide and 1-inch-thick strips
3 tablespoons olive oil
½ cup white wine
1 scant teaspoon salt
½ medium onion, finely chopped
1 tablespoon chopped parsley
2 tablespoons butter

Flatten the meat with a cleaver to ¾-inch thickness. Combine the oil, wine, salt, onion, and parsley in a pottery or enameled bowl; add the meat and let marinate for several hours. Remove meat from marinade. Melt butter in a heavy skillet and fry lamb until golden brown on both sides. This can be served with mint jelly, if you like it with your lamb.

CUCUMBER, ONION, AND TOMATO SALAD

3 cups thinly sliced cucumbers (if waxed, peel first)
1 cup thinly sliced red onions
2 cups thinly sliced tomatoes
1 cup olive oil
1 cup cider vinegar
½ cup sugar
1 teaspoon salt
Freshly ground pepper to taste

Arrange the sliced cucumbers, onions, and tomatoes in a flat serving dish. Combine the remaining ingredients, shaking well to dissolve the sugar. Pour over the vegetables and marinate for 2 hours. To serve, arrange on salad plates, or in individual wood salad bowls, with some of the dressing.

FRENCH GOOSE (ROASTED PIG'S STOMACH)
COLE SLAW (PAGE 50)   COCONUT CREAM PIE

French goose was my mother's name for stuffed, roasted pig's stomach, a very old Pennsylvania Dutch recipe that looks and tastes a lot better than it sounds. The sausage flavoring goes through the vegetables, and the trick is in cutting them so they are all different shapes and sizes—rounds of carrot, half-moon slices of celery, and diced potatoes—then when you slice it you have a pretty, colorful kind of design. I did this once for a food show on the Main Line. I knew when I brought it out they would all have a fit—and they did, but the minute they saw it sliced they changed their minds. I sometimes serve this for the Wednesday night dinners and I get away with it by not telling the guests what they are going to have, just bringing in the roasted stomach sliced. Once they taste it, they love it.

If you can't get a pig's stomach (often you can find them sold as hog maws in southern or black markets), you can use one of those roaster bags, the clear plastic-film bags sold for sealing and cooking roasts and chickens, piercing the bottom in a couple of places to let the fat out. This won't have the shape, texture, or appearance of the pig's stomach, but it works pretty well.

FRENCH GOOSE (ROASTED PIG'S STOMACH)

    1 pig's stomach
    2 pounds fresh pork sausage meat
    2 pounds white potatoes, peeled and diced
    8 medium stalks of celery, sliced crosswise
  ½ pound carrots, peeled and sliced
    3 tablespoons chopped parsley
    1 small onion, chopped fine (optional)
    1 teaspoon salt
  ⅛ teaspoon freshly ground pepper

Wash the pig's stomach well. Combine the sausage meat, vegetables, and seasonings, mixing well. Stuff the pig's stomach with this mixture, stuffing it as tightly and full as you can. Close the openings with baking nails and string.

Place the stuffed stomach on a rack in a covered roaster and bake in a 350° oven for approximately 3 hours. Remove roaster cover and baste roast with the drippings that have oozed out. Increase oven heat to 375° and cook until golden brown, about 20 minutes. To serve, put on a board or platter and cut in 2-inch-thick slices—no thinner, or it will fall apart.

COCONUT CREAM PIE

    2 cups milk
  ⅔ cup sugar
  ½ teaspoon salt
    3 tablespoons cornstarch
    2 eggs, separated
  1½ tablespoons butter
    1 teaspoon vanilla
  1¼ cups shredded coconut
       9-inch baked pie shell
       Pinch of cream of tartar
    4 tablespoons sugar

Scald 1½ cups milk in the top of a double boiler. Combine the ⅔ cup sugar, salt, and cornstarch with the remaining ½ cup milk, mixing to a paste. Add to the hot milk and cook, stirring, until thickened.

Beat the egg yolks, add a small amount of the hot milk mixture, and blend. Pour into the hot milk mixture and cook 2 minutes. Remove from the heat and mix in the butter, vanilla, and ¾ cup of the coconut. Cool, and pour into the baked pie shell.

Beat the egg whites with the cream of tartar until they hold soft peaks; then beat in the 4 tablespoons sugar, and continue to beat until stiff and glossy. Cover the pie filling with this meringue and sprinkle with the remaining ½ cup coconut. Bake in a 350° oven for 5 minutes, or until meringue is a delicate golden brown.

BREADS

I've had people ask me how we can find time to bake bread for the restaurant. It really doesn't take that long—most of the time is in the rising—and it is worth it, because homemade bread is so different, not just in the taste, but the texture.

BASIC WHITE BREAD

2 cups scalded milk
3 tablespoons sugar
1 tablespoon salt
2 tablespoons butter
2 packages dry granular yeast or 2 yeast cakes dissolved
        in 1/4 cup lukewarm water (110° to 115°)
7 cups sifted all-purpose flour

Cool the milk to lukewarm. Add the sugar, salt, and butter. Let the yeast proof (form tiny bubbles on the surface, which shows it is active) and add to the milk. Combine with the flour and mix thoroughly; then knead vigorously on a lightly floured surface, or in an electric mixer with a dough hook, until the dough is smooth and elastic to the touch. Put in a greased bowl, turning dough so it is greased on all sides, cover with a damp cloth, and let it rise in a warm, draft-free spot until double in bulk. Cut or punch down the dough and knead a little more. Divide dough into 3 parts, shape each one into a loaf, and place in greased loaf pans. Cover with a cloth and let rise in a warm place until doubled in bulk. Bake in a 375° oven for 35 minutes.

Ours is a very informal, family-style business
where everyone pitches in and takes over any job that needs doing.
Waitress Lena Fisher doubles as our breadmaker,
five days a week.

PECAN RAISIN BREAD

Use basic white bread recipe. After first rising, punch dough down and work in 1 cup pecan nutmeats and 1 cup raisins. Cream ⅓ cup sugar and 1 egg and work this into the dough. Let rise until double in bulk and proceed as for basic bread.

WHOLE WHEAT BREAD

Use basic white bread recipe, substituting whole wheat flour for half the white flour, and add ¼ cup honey to the milk mixture.

BLANCHE FRANKEHOUSER'S OLD-FASHIONED OATMEAL BREAD

  2 cups boiling water
  1 cup rolled oats
  ⅓ cup butter
  ½ cup light molasses
  4 teaspoons salt
  2 packages dry granular yeast
  2 eggs
 5½ cups sifted all-purpose flour

Combine the boiling water, rolled oats, butter, molasses, and salt. Cool mixture to lukewarm; then add the yeast. Mix well. Blend in the eggs and stir in the flour. The dough will be softer than a kneaded dough. Place dough in a greased bowl, cover, and store in the refrigerator at least 2 hours, or until needed.

Remove chilled dough and knead about five times (this helps to remove the air). Shape into two loaves on a well-floured surface, place in greased pans, and cover with a cloth.

Let rise in a warm place until double in bulk, about 2 hours.
Bake in a 375° oven for 1 hour.

CORN BREAD

1½ cups yellow cornmeal
1 cup all-purpose flour
⅓ cup sugar
1 teaspoon salt
1 tablespoon baking powder
⅔ cup butter
2 eggs
1½ cups milk

Sift together the cornmeal, flour, sugar, salt, and baking powder. Cream the butter and beat in the eggs. Add the sifted dry ingredients to the creamed butter alternately with the milk. Do not overbeat. Mix just until well blended. Pour into a greased 9-inch-square cake pan. Bake in a 375° oven for 40 minutes. Serve warm, with butter.

RAISED MUFFINS

2 tablespoons butter
⅓ cup sugar
1 teaspoon salt
1 cup scalded milk
¾ cup boiling water
1 package granular dry yeast
1 egg, slightly beaten
3½ cups all-purpose flour

Add the butter, sugar and salt to the milk and water. Cool to lukewarm; then add the yeast. When yeast is dissolved, add the egg. Sift in the flour, mixing thoroughly. Cover and let rise until double in bulk. Fill buttered muffin pans ⅔ full and let dough rise until it comes to the top of the pans. Bake in a 375° oven for 30 minutes.

PUMPKIN DESSERT BREAD

    3 cups flour
    1 teaspoon salt
    2 cups sugar
    4 eggs, beaten
 1¼ cups salad oil
  ½ cup nutmeats
    1 teaspoon baking soda
    3 teaspoons cinnamon
    2 cups cooked, strained pumpkin or canned pumpkin

Combine the flour, salt, and sugar in a large mixing bowl. Make a well in the center with a wooden spoon and add all the remaining ingredients. Stir carefully, just enough to dampen the dry ingredients. Pour into 2 greased loaf pans and bake in a 350° oven for 1 hour.

Poor Mans Pound Cake
Take 1 cup of sugar   1 cup of thick milk
1½ tablespoon full of butter   2 eggs
1 teaspoonful of saleratus   2 teaspoonful of
creamatartar and some nutmeg   1 tin
ful of flour

CHAPTER IV

Memory Foods

WE ALL HAVE taste memories from our childhood that we carry through the years of special goodies our mothers and grandmothers used to make. You'll find that you never really experience the same flavor until you make them yourself, trying to recollect and reconstruct exactly how they were done, and the little tricks and techniques you noted almost subconsciously.

I've had people say to me, "Oh yes, I remember that. How

good it was," but they don't know how to make it. If you don't keep on making these memory foods, as I call them, and showing your children how, they will be lost, and soon all they will be *is* a memory.

That's why I'm including some of the old recipes I loved as a child. A few of them, like the lemonade and sugar cookies and candy, I still make for my own children. Others, such as the homemade potato chips and egg cheese, I hadn't done in years—and I found I needed a little help with them.

LEMONADE AND SUGAR COOKIES

I remember that when I was a little girl, my grandmother always provided lemonade and sugar cookies in the hot weather for the thrashing parties. At ten o'clock and three o'clock it would be my job to take out to the men working in the fields the enameled bucket of lemonade with a big block of ice in it, and a shiny new tin cup. If there was any left, I could have it; so you can be sure I managed to take the bucket away before it had all been drunk.

Aunt Suie would take a wooden stomper and stomp the sugar into the lemon slices in the bucket; then she'd add the water and squeeze in more lemon juice and grate nutmeg on the top. Somehow that little bit of nutmeg seemed to bring out the greatest flavor in the lemonade, though it did look a bit funny. The first time I made it after we were married, Abe thought I'd got dirt in the lemonade. The stomping was important, because it mingled the lemon juice and sugar and flattened the slices so they floated to the top and stayed there. Always with lemonade we had what we called peppernut cookies, very soft sugar cookies with a raisin in the center.

LEMONADE

5 lemons
1 cup granulated sugar
1 gallon water
1 quart ice cubes
   Grated nutmeg
   Mint sprigs

Squeeze 3 lemons and reserve the juice. Slice the remaining lemons ¼ inch thick and press them into ½ cup of the sugar, using a wooden mallet or old-fashioned wooden potato masher. Do this in the bucket or container you will serve the lemonade in. Let the slices stand in the sugar for 15 minutes; then add the water, the reserved lemon juice, and the remaining sugar. Stir until sugar is well dissolved; then add the ice cubes and grate fresh nutmeg on the top. Garnish with sprigs of fresh mint.

*Lemonade and sugar cookies down by the old spring house—
that's real memory food.*

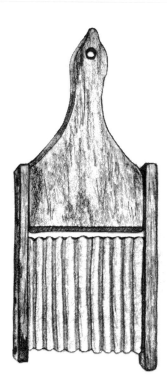

The old-fashioned kitchen tools shown here and all through the book are from the great collection of my friend, Kitty Brown. Some of them are as good today as they ever were. The three-gallon stoneware crock is the kind we used for sauerkraut or canned sausage. The crinkle-cutter slices French fries and the food mill purees fruits and vegetables. The thing that looks like a piece of Swiss cheese is a "humane" mouse trap that snares but doesn't harm the mice; it's still being made, I believe.

PEPPERNUT OR SUGAR COOKIES

¼ pound butter
2 tablespoons margarine
1⅓ cups granulated sugar
2 eggs
¾ cup buttermilk
1 teaspoon baking soda, dissolved in 1 tablespoon boiling
    water
1 teaspoon vanilla
3 cups flour
1 teaspoon baking powder
½ teaspoon nutmeg
¼ teaspoon salt
¼ cup raisins

Cream the butter, margarine, and sugar together until light and fluffy. Beat in the eggs, one at a time, beating lightly. Add the buttermilk, dissolved soda, and vanilla.

Sift together the flour, baking powder, nutmeg, and salt. Mix into the first mixture. When well blended, refrigerate for 30 minutes. Preheat the oven to 350°.

Drop the cooky mixture by teaspoonfuls onto a greased cooky sheet, spacing them at least 2 inches apart as they will spread out and flatten as they cook. Place a raisin in the center of each cookie and bake at 350° for 15 minutes, or until very light brown. Do not let them get too dark. This makes about 3 dozen cookies.

Note: If the batter is too thin, add ¼ cup more flour, blending well.

RASPBERRY SHRUB

Another of our hot weather drinks was raspberry shrub, which we made with the black raspberries we picked along the banks of the streams. Raspberry shrub is a very old recipe; you find it in the eighteenth- and nineteenth-century cookbooks. In those days, they believed you should take vinegar to quench your thirst. Actually, if you drink water in very hot weather, you soon get thirsty again; but stir in some raspberry shrub and you'll find it really works.

COUSIN ELIZABETH DENLINGER'S RASPBERRY SHRUB

1 quart black raspberries
1 pint cider vinegar

Combine the raspberries and vinegar and let stand overnight. Next day, strain and measure the juice. To each pint of juice add 1 pound of granulated sugar.

Boil 10 minutes; then put in jars and seal. Use one-third glass of this concentrate, and fill the glass up with ice-cold water.

Note: Raspberry shrub is also delicious on desserts like tapioca pudding or angel food cake, or you can stir it into ice cream.

195

EGG CHEESE

We Pennsylvania Dutch have always been noted for our home-made schmierkase (cottage cheese), cup cheese, ball cheese, and egg cheese.

Egg cheese, with homemade bread and a good mild barrel molasses, was something we had for breakfast or as a snack when we came home from school, maybe with a mug of hot chocolate. Egg cheese is a little like ricotta, very light and creamy, just firm enough to cut with a cheese knife. You slice it down, lay it on the bread, and dribble molasses over it; when you eat it, your fingers get good and sticky, which is part of the fun.

People in Lancaster County prided themselves on the lightness of their egg cheese, and they drained and shaped it in special heart-shaped pierced tin molds. The antique molds now fetch up to $50 or $60, but you get just the same result if you use a wicker or pottery coeur à la crème mold. A friend of mine made a mold from a coffee can, piercing the bottom with his own design.

LANCASTER COUNTY EGG CHEESE

2 quarts sweet milk
6 eggs
2 cups buttermilk
1 teaspoon salt
2 teaspoons sugar

Warm the sweet milk. Beat the eggs until fluffy and add the buttermilk, salt, and sugar. Beat slightly and pour slowly into the warm milk. Cover the pan with the lid and let stand for several minutes on medium-low heat, stirring only occasionally.

Remove the lid and watch for the curds (the cheese) and whey to separate. Immediately spoon the curds lightly into a pierced mold, using a slotted spoon, and leave to cool and drain (balance the mold on a bowl into which the liquid can drip). It is the gentle spooning into the mold that prevents the cheese getting solid and heavy. If you drop it into a sieve, it will get as heavy as lead. It should be removed very delicately from the pan and just laid in the mold.

When cold and drained, unmold the cheese onto a dish and serve with bread and molasses. This makes enough for 8 servings.

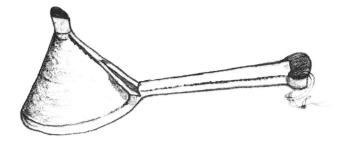

SALSIFY CASSEROLE

———————

Salsify, a long, white root vegetable shaped rather like a carrot, is called oyster plant in the country areas, because it does taste like oysters. In the old days, when oysters were very difficult to get, the oyster plant was baked in a casserole, just like scalloped oysters.

We brought the salsify in late in the fall and stored it in a cool part of the cellar in a tub, covered with dirt—a layer of salsify, then a layer of dirt. That way it would keep at least until January. This recipe comes from my husband's mother.

MOTHER GROFF'S SALSIFY CASSEROLE

    1 pound salsify
    1 cup bread crumbs
    1 cup small oyster crackers
      Salt, freshly ground pepper
    ½ cup melted butter
    1 cup light cream

Wash and scrape the salsify and cook in salted water until tender. Slice ½ inch thick. Line a buttered casserole with ¼ cup bread crumbs, add half the salsify, sprinkle with salt and pepper, top with ½ cup bread crumbs, ¼ cup butter and the oyster crackers. Pour the cream over this, then add the rest of the salsify, sprinkle with the remaining crumbs and butter, and bake in a 375° oven for 35 minutes. Serves 4.

POTATO CHIPS

How many people today would ever dream of making their own potato chips, when it is so easy to buy them in the supermarket? Yet homemade potato chips are something else; they have a completely different taste from the store-bought kind.

We used to make potato chips for special company dinners and weddings, but I hadn't thought of it for years, until I came to test them for a dinner I wanted to put in this book.

I had a bag of good mealy potatoes and my mother's recipe, and it looked like plain sailing. I sliced the potatoes as thin as a penny, exactly the way I remembered from when I was nine years old and watched mother, and dropped them in fat of just the right temperature—and all I got was something that looked like limp white dishcloths; they never did get golden and crisp as they should. No way could I get those things right. I used up a five-pound bag of potatoes trying. Mother was sick at the time and I didn't want to bother her; so I called my neighbor and asked if she knew anything about making potato chips. She said she'd never done it, but she knew you had to have a certain type of potato, an Irish Cobbler, and that the potatoes shouldn't get too cold.

Finally, I had to call a friend of mine at the potato chip

200

factory and ask him what the secret was. My neighbor was right about the potatoes not getting too cold. Cold affects them, and if the mineral line around the inside of the skin starts to get brown, you might as well give up; you'll never get crisp, golden potato chips. In the factory, the potatoes are stored at a controlled temperature of 52°, and here was I trying to make them in January, with the temperature well below freezing.

My friend volunteered to bring me what I needed, and he came flying out of his car into the house with five potatoes wrapped like babies in layers of newspaper so they wouldn't get nipped by the cold.

The very first chip came out golden and perfect. I didn't lose one. It was all in the potatoes, and here I'd wasted six hours fooling around trying to do the impossible.

HOMEMADE POTATO CHIPS

2 pounds Irish Cobbler potatoes (kept at a temperature of 52 degrees)
2 cups peanut oil
  Salt

Wash and peel the potatoes. Slice them as thin as a penny (Mother used an old-fashioned adjustable cutting board, and you can get a similar type in kitchen equipment stores, called a mandoline cutter), and immediately drop into ice water to stop them turning pink.

Heat the oil to 360°. Dry the chips on paper towels and fry until golden brown and crisp. Remove, drain on paper towels, and salt lightly.

Note: Chips fried in oil will keep in an airtight tin for months. If you use lard, you have to eat them the same day.

PUFFED POTATOES

My friend, Kitty Brown, told me about this way of doing potatoes, which I often make as a snack in the evening before bedtime. In the old days of coal stoves, when the fire was burning up before being banked for the night, sliced potatoes were put directly on the hot stovetop, cooked until crisp and puffy, and eaten with butter and salt. In Kitty s updated version, you cut the well-washed potatoes in 3 strips an inch thick, with the peel on, and bake them at 450° until they get real crisp and puff up into blisters on the outside, with the inside flaky. Puncture the blisters with a fork and put some butter in the hole; salt the potatoes and eat while hot.

CANDY

Candy making is another thing I learned from my mother. When I married and was casting around for something to do that would bring people to the farm, the first thing I thought of was making candy.

When I married Abe, my father told me that if you wanted to keep a man happy, you should let him go hunting once a year; he and Daddy even went hunting the last three days of our honeymoon, and that time I went along too. The next year, when Abe and Daddy took off the first week in December to hunt deer, Mother went along with them to do the cooking, and I stayed home to make candy. Mother had given me her recipes, but she didn't think from the little experience I'd had as a child that I could do it on my own. Were they surprised when they came home and found that in four days I'd hand-coated 100 pounds of candy! I got up at 5:00 every morning and worked until 11:00 at night. In two weeks all the candy was gone, everyone came and bought it. I might have gone on making candy, but Daddy talked me out of it; so I started the restaurant instead.

I don't have too much time now to make chocolate-coated creams, but I do make butter mints for company dinners and the simple, old-fashioned taffy and brittle the children like.

BUTTER MINTS

4 tablespoons butter
1 pound confectioners' sugar
8 drops oil of peppermint
2 tablespoons cold water

Melt the butter; stir in the sugar, oil of peppermint, and water. Knead until smooth and firm. At this point, you can knead in a few drops of food coloring, for colored mints. Red doesn't work well; somehow the alcohol in the mint seems to fade it out.

Press the mint mixture into desired shapes. The simplest way is to form it into balls, roll them out, and make a criss-cross pattern on the top with a fork. Or you can put the mixture through a cooky press. I use the star shape and put in half blue and half white mint mixture, for a blue and white star. This makes about 1½ pounds of mints.

AUNT MIRIAM'S SHELLBARK TAFFY

1½ cups granulated sugar
1 cup water
⅓ cup cider vinegar
3 tablespoons molasses
½ cup shellbarks (similar to hickory nuts, or use other nuts
such as walnuts, almonds, hazelnuts, peanuts)

Combine the sugar, water, vinegar, and molasses in a saucepan. Bring to a boil and boil to the hard-crack stage (taffy goes hard when dropped in cold water), or 300° on a candy thermometer.

Put the nuts in a buttered 9-inch-square cake pan, almost covering the bottom, and pour the taffy over them. Cool at room temperature and mark in squares. Makes about 1½ pounds of taffy.

OLD-FASHIONED PEANUT BRITTLE

2 cups granulated sugar
3 cups white corn syrup
  Pinch of salt
3 cups raw peanuts
1 teaspoon baking soda

Use a 10-inch iron skillet to make the brittle. Make a circle of the sugar in the skillet and put the syrup and salt in the center. Starting with the skillet on a cold burner, turn the heat to medium-high, add the peanuts, and cook for 8 minutes. Reduce heat to medium-low and cook for 16 minutes, stirring continually. Remove from heat and stir in the baking soda.

Grease a 14 x 17-inch cooky sheet or a marble slab with butter. Pour on the brittle and leave to set. When set, score into 2-inch squares. Break when cool. Cover tightly with plastic wrap and store in an airtight container. This makes about 36 squares.

Bender Candy
1 lb granulated sugar ¼ lb glucose ¼ pt. water
1 teaspoon parafine flavor to suit taste

CHAPTER V

Keeping Foods

THERE'S nothing quite as gratifying as going to your pantry or cellar shelf in midwinter and picking out a jar of fruit or pickles that you put up yourself. When you can your own produce, you know how fresh it is. As Mother always said, "Nothing comes out of a jar better than what you put in." In other words, don't use inferior fruits and vegetables; that's false economy. Only the best and freshest are worth the effort.

Canning and preserving can be an art. If you take the

206

trouble to pack your fruits and pickles beautifully in the jars, they are as much a pleasure to look at as to eat. Few sights are more appetizing and tempting than row upon row of jars of brilliant chow chow and pepper relish, translucent watermelon rind, snowy pickled cauliflower, smooth pale yellow Bartlett pears and golden peaches, and rich red beets—and you have the glow of pride and achievement that comes from knowing you did it all yourself.

I have always made pickles and preserves, mincemeat and apple butter, and I always will. Not just because we serve them in the restaurant but, more importantly, because nothing to me is more fun than getting together with my family and helpers and friends and putting up all that glorious fresh produce. It's like having your garden in the bank.

FREEZING

Since we Pennsylvania Dutch got freezers, there's much less canning than in the old days. Certain things—for instance, delicate tender young vegetables like corn, green peas, and lima beans—are, to my mind, much better frozen than canned.

It is most important to have the vegetables in the freezer 3 to 4 hours after they are picked. That way they retain their freshness and flavor. Clean, trim, and thoroughly wash the vegetables before blanching and freezing them.

For peas and lima beans, shell the vegetables, drop them in boiling water, and boil 1 minute after the water returns to the boil. Remove, drain, and immediately immerse in cold water. Continue to change the water as it gets warm until the vegetables are thoroughly cold. Drain and place in freezer bags or boxes. The quicker they hit the freezer, the better.

Corn frozen on the cob is a waste of time, space, and corn. After it is thawed, it has no flavor whatsoever. By far the best way is to parboil the cob and cut the corn off very quickly.

FROZEN CORN

Corn for freezing should be freshly picked, preferably early in the morning when it is full of flavor. Husk and silk each ear and when you are almost finished, put on two large pots, each two-thirds full of water, and bring to a rolling boil. Drop in enough ears to fill each pot and when the water comes back to the boil, cook for no more than three minutes, or just until no milk comes out when you pierce a kernel with the point of a sharp knife. Immediately remove the ears and immerse in a sink full of cold water. In two minutes, drain off the water and cover the corn with fresh cold water. Repeat this process until the corn and the cob are completely cold.

Drain the corn and cut off the kernels with a very sharp paring knife or the corn-cutting board sold in hardware and kitchen equipment stores (the board has an attachment for creaming corn, which is handy if you want to make creamed corn, corn fritters, or corn pudding). I prefer to use the knife. Cut close to the cob and toward you; then use the back of the knife in the opposite direction to strip the remainder of the corn, the milky part, from the cob. That way you won't dull your knife edge by using it the wrong way. It's amazing how fast the edge goes. When we cut off corn, Abe comes in every twenty minutes or so to sharpen the knives.

Put the corn kernels into freezer bags or boxes immediately. To reheat frozen corn, put it in a heavy pan with ¼ cup water and remove from the heat as soon as it has thawed and warmed through.

Canning is to me like having your garden in the bank.

FROZEN BERRIES

When I freeze berries—raspberries, blackberries, blueberries, and similar soft, perishable fruits—I never wash them, because I have found this gives them freezer burn. I just put them in bags and freeze them loose. To thaw, I put them in a colander and run water over them, which both defrosts and washes them. Then all I have to do is mix them with the glaze and they are all ready for a fresh berry pie.

With strawberries, I leave the stems on and freeze the berries individually on a cooky sheet, then when they are frozen solid, pop them in freezer bags or boxes.

CANNING, PICKLING, AND PRESERVING

Home canning is really very simple. Although at first it may seem rather an expense to invest in all those jars and a home canner, which is a deep pot fitted with a rack to hold 7 quart jars or 12 pint jars, remember that you will be using them over and over again for years. You can use any big deep pot and put a rack inside, but the canner is a good investment. It doesn't cost much and you can also use it for cooking corn, steaming clams, or any kind of quantity cooking. The rack has handles, so it is easy to lower and lift the jars.

The technique of canning is simple, once you get used to it. First sterilize your quart or pint jars for 15 minutes in boiling water, leaving them in the water with the heat off until you are ready to drain and use them. You can also sterilize them by leaving them in a 250° oven for 20 to 25 minutes. Be sure the jars are hot when you pack them, as the heat ensures that they seal properly. The best and safest jar to use is the type with a vacuum-seal flat lid and a screw-on ring cover that fits over it. Don't boil the lid, which has a rubber seal around the inside; just pour boiling water over it and leave in the water until ready to use.

Drain, fill, and seal the sterilized jars. Most home-canning booklets tell you to leave 1-inch head space for starchy foods (corn, beans, peas) and ½-inch head space for other fruits and vegetables, but I usually find it works best to fill the jars to the neck only. I also like to start the canning from cool water, rather than putting the jars into boiling water, as most booklets recommend. I lower the jars on the rack into the canner, add enough water to come to the neck of the jars, bring this to a boil and boil for the required time with the cover on. This is known as the cold-pack method.

Because of the acid reaction of the vinegar in pickling, use crocks or containers of pottery, stoneware, enamel, or glass to hold the pickles and stainless steel or enamel pots for cooking. Be sure the pot is big enough for the quantity you are going to prepare. For chow chow you would need an 8 to 10-quart pot, which is a good basic size.

For transferring pickles to the jars, use glass or stainless steel measuring cups, slotted enamel, stainless or wooden spoons, and enameled ladles, plus a wide-mouthed funnel for filling jars with liquid. For preserves, you'll need a 6 to 8-quart preserving kettle with a lid.

Sterilize the jars and the lids as described above and leave in the water until you are ready for them. When the food is ready to jar, lift the jars from the water with metal tongs, drain well and stand upright on a board or any surface that won't be harmed by heat or spills. Fill each jar to within $\frac{1}{4}$ inch of the top, wipe the edge clean, then seal quickly and tightly with the lid and ring.

Let the jars cool overnight. Next morning, test for leakage by turning each jar upside down. If the seal is not completely airtight, the food will spoil.

CANNED FRUITS

Fruits are canned in a sugar-and-water syrup. I like to use a thick syrup of 1 part sugar to 1 part water. Cook until the sugar is dissolved, and bring to a boil.

To prepare Bartlett pears, core and peel with a sharp knife (I find a knife gives a smoother result than a vegetable peeler), leaving the stems on.

*After we finish canning, the stocks in the cellar
will keep the restaurant supplied for another year.*

For peaches, the skins should be removed. Blanch in boiling water for 1 or 2 minutes, drain, cover with cold water to stop the fruit cooking, and strip off the skins. Leave the fruit whole, or cut in halves, as you prefer. You may leave the skins on apricots.

Cherries don't need peeling, but sour cherries should be pitted. Sweet cherries need not be pitted. If I have large Bing cherries, I like to leave the stems on; they look much prettier when you serve them. Any fruit that hasn't been peeled or pitted should be punctured with a fork to stop the skin from bursting during the processing.

Pack the fruit in the sterilized jars and add enough syrup to fill the jar to the neck. (Some people like to put 1 pit in the jar with the peaches to strengthen the flavor.) Before sealing, release any air that may be trapped in the liquid by running a long, thin rubber spatula down between the inside of the jar and the fruit, moving the fruit around slightly to let the air out.

Wipe the tops of the jars, seal with vacuum lids and covers, and process by the cold-pack method for 15 minutes, timing after the water comes to a boil.

CANNED MEATS

In the days before freezers, we preserved our meats in the fall and winter, after butchering, by canning. Fatty things like sausage were fried down and put in a crock, covered with clear lard. We'd have crocks of sausage and spareribs, quarts of canned chicken, beef, pork loin, and tenderloin. Daddy butchered all winter; so then we had fresh meat, but in the summer we'd have our canned beefsteaks and pork loin.

I don't suppose anyone would go to the trouble of canning meats now that there are freezers, but until I opened the restaurant, where we serve ribs of beef, I still canned beefsteaks. Here's how to do it, in case you're interested.

Take 2 pounds of front-quarter Delmonico steak and pack into a sterilized quart jar. Add 1 teaspoon salt to each quart jar of raw meat. Seal the jars and process by the cold-pack method, starting with cool water and boiling for 2½ hours after the water comes to a boil. The method and timing is the same for all meats, except hamburger, which takes only 2 hours. You can get a 3½-pound frying chicken, without the back, into a quart jar.

DILL PICKLES

Dill pickles, which take only 5 minutes canning time, are one of the easiest things to start with, if you have never canned before—and are they good! Put up in pint jars, they make great small gifts.

> 4 medium-sized pickling cucumbers (about 3 inches long)
> 1 tablespoon dill seed
> ½ tablespoon mustard seed
> ½ teaspoon minced garlic
> ¾ cup cider vinegar
> ¾ cup water
> 1½ tablespoons salt

Wash the cucumbers and cut in quarters lengthwise. Arrange the strips in a sterilized quart canning jar and add the dill seed, mustard seed, and garlic.

Combine vinegar, water, and salt in an enameled or stainless steel saucepan and bring to a boil. Pour over the cucumbers. Seal jars with lids and covers and process in the canner for 5 minutes, timing from the moment the water comes to a full boil. Makes 1 quart.

SPICED CANTALOUPE

2-pound firm ripe cantaloupe
⅔ cup sugar
⅓ cup water
3 tablespoons cider vinegar
3 drops oils of cinnamon and cloves (equal parts)

The oils of cinnamon and cloves can be bought at a drugstore. The oils are preferable to ground spices, as they keep the melon from discoloring.

Wash the cantaloupe, cut in 1-inch-thick slices, and remove seeds and rind. Cut cantaloupe flesh into 2-inch pieces and pack them into a 1-quart sterilized jar.

Combine the sugar, water, vinegar, and oils of cinnamon and cloves in a stainless steel or enameled saucepan and bring to a boil, stirring until the sugar dissolves. Pour this syrup into the jar over the cantaloupe, filling the jar to the neck. Place self-sealing lid and cover on jar and process in the home canner for 15 minutes, timing from the moment the water comes to a full boil. Makes 1 quart.

SPICED WATERMELON RIND

5 pounds watermelon rind (leave on about ¼-inch of the
pink flesh, for color)
½ cup salt
2 quarts water
2½ pounds sugar
2 cups cider vinegar
1 cup water
⅛ teaspoon oils of cinnamon and cloves (equal parts)

Cut the watermelon rind in 2-inch pieces. Mix the salt and the 2 quarts water and pour over the rind. Leave to soak overnight.

Next day, drain and rinse in cold water. Drain again. Cook in water until rind is tender, and turns translucent. Drain.

Combine the sugar, cider vinegar, 1 cup water, and oils of cinnamon and cloves in a stainless steel or enameled saucepan and bring to a boil, stirring until sugar dissolves.

Pour this syrup over the drained rind and let stand overnight. Next morning, drain off the syrup, cook it for several minutes, and again pour over the rind. Repeat this process of soaking, draining, and soaking for 3 days. (This long process makes the rind clear.)

On the third day, cook the rind in the syrup for 3 minutes. Pour into hot sterilized pint or quart jars and seal. Makes 6 quarts or 12 pints.

MUSTARD PICKLES

  3 quarts cider vinegar
  1 quart water
  1 cup ground mustard
  1 tablespoon saccharine
  6 tablespoons alum
  7 tablespoons whole allspice
½ cup salt
  5 quarts tiny pickling cucumbers, about 2 inches long

Combine the vinegar, water, mustard, saccharine, alum, allspice, and salt. Put the cucumbers in a large enameled pot, pour the mixture over them, and bring to a boil. When hot, pack in hot sterilized jars and seal. Makes about 7 quarts.

Note: The saccharine reacts with the pickles, keeping them green, while the alum keeps their crispness.

SEVEN-DAY SWEET PICKLES

7 pounds medium-sized pickling cucumbers (about 3 inches long)
1 quart cider vinegar
8 cups sugar
2 tablespoons salt
2 tablespoons mixed pickling spices

Wash the cucumbers, put them in a large container, and cover with boiling water. Allow to stand for 24 hours. Drain.

Repeat this process each day for four days, using fresh boiling water each time.

On the fifth day, slice the cucumbers in ¼-inch rings. Combine the vinegar, sugar, salt, and pickling spices in a stainless steel or enameled pan. Bring to a boil and pour over the sliced cucumbers. Let stand 24 hours.

On the sixth day, drain off the syrup, bring to a boil, and pour over the cucumbers.

On the seventh day, drain off and boil the syrup once more. Add the cucumbers and bring to the boiling point. Pack into hot sterilized jars and seal. Makes about 7 pints.

PICKLED CAULIFLOWER

4 medium heads cauliflower
4 cups sugar
2 cups cider vinegar
1 cup water
1 teaspoon mustard seed
½ teaspoon turmeric
½ teaspoon celery seed

Clean the cauliflower and break the heads into buds. Cook in salted water to cover until just tender, approximately 7 minutes. Drain.

Put the sugar, vinegar, water, mustard seed, turmeric, and celery seed in an enameled or stainless steel pan and bring to a boil, stirring until the sugar dissolves. Add the drained cauliflower and boil 2 minutes. Pack into hot sterilized jars and seal. Makes 6 pints or 3 quarts.

Note: If this is not packed in jars, it will keep in a covered container in the refrigerator for 4 weeks.

PEPPER RELISH

1½ cups chopped red peppers
1½ cups chopped green peppers
  1 cup chopped onion
  2 teaspoons salt
  2 cups sugar
  1 cup cider vinegar
  2 tablespoons mustard seed
  1 tablespoon celery seed

Put the peppers and onion in a pan with water to cover and 1 teaspoon of the salt. Cook until tender but still crisp, and drain well.

Combine the sugar, vinegar, mustard and celery seeds, and remaining teaspoon salt in an enameled or stainless steel saucepan and bring to a boil, stirring until the sugar dissolves. Pour over the drained peppers and onions, return to the pan, bring to a boil and cook 2 minutes. Pour into hot sterilized quart jars and seal. Makes about 2 quarts.

Note: If you don't want to pack the relish in jars, it will keep in a covered container, under refrigeration, for 3 to 4 weeks. Packed in small jars, the relish makes a good gift.

PICKLED BEETS

      5 pounds fresh beets
      1 cup sugar
      1 cup cider vinegar
      1 cup beet broth
      2 cups water
      3 teaspoons salt
   1½ teaspoons pepper

Wash but do not peel the beets. Cover with water and boil until tender. Drain, reserving 1 cup of the beet liquid. Peel beets and cut or slice the size you desire.

Put the sugar, vinegar, beet broth, water, salt, and pepper in an enameled or stainless steel saucepan and heat, stirring until the sugar dissolves. Add the sliced beets, bring to a boil and boil 2 minutes. Pack into hot sterilized quart jars, and seal. Makes 3 quarts.

CHOW CHOW

   1 cup dried navy beans (Great Northern), washed and
         picked over
   2 cups dried red kidney beans, washed and picked over
   2 cups lima beans
   2 cups string beans, trimmed, washed, and cut in 1-inch
         pieces
   1 cup yellow wax beans, trimmed, washed, and cut in 1-inch
         pieces
   2 cups cauliflower buds
   2 cups coarsely chopped celery
   2 cups coarsely chopped red and green peppers
   2 cups sliced carrots
   2 cups fresh corn kernels, cut off the cob
   2 cups tiny white onions, peeled
   2 cups chopped cabbage
   2 cups chopped sweet gherkins
   5 cups sugar

2½ cups cider vinegar
1½ cups water
2 tablespoons mustard seed
1 tablespoon celery seed
1 teaspoon turmeric

When I make chow chow, I like to cook the vegetables individually, so each one keeps its color and does not become overcooked. This may sound like a long, tedious process, but it really isn't, if you cook the vegetables one after another in a big pot, draining them and layering them in a large dish pan.

Bring the dried navy and kidney beans to a boil in water to cover by at least 2 inches. Boil uncovered for 2 minutes; then turn off the heat and let the beans soak for 1 hour.

Bring the water to a boil again, reduce the heat and simmer partially covered until tender, about 1 hour. Add more liquid if it is needed. Drain the beans and set aside.

While the dried beans are cooking, bring 4 quarts of water to a boil in a 6-quart pot. Drop in the lima beans and when the water returns to a boil, cook until tender, but still crisp, about 20 to 30 minutes. Scoop the beans out of the water with a slotted spoon or sieve and run cold water over them for a minute or two to stop the cooking and preserve the color. Drain and transfer to the dish pan. Cook all the other vegetables (except the gherkins, which do not require cooking) in the same manner, cooking only until they are tender-crisp.

Make layers of all the vegetables and the cooked dried beans in the dish pan.

Combine the sugar, vinegar, water, mustard seed, celery seed, and turmeric in a 10-quart pot and bring to a boil, stirring until the sugar dissolves. Pour all the vegetables from the dish pan into the pot and boil in the syrup for 5 minutes. Stir gently with a wooden spoon, stirring only enough to mix. Do not mash or break the vegetables. Ladle into hot sterilized pint or quart jars and seal. Makes 5 quarts or 10 pints.

LETE'S SAUERKRAUT

Finely shred 1 small head of cabbage and pack in a sterilized quart jar. Sprinkle 1 teaspoon salt on top and fill the jar to the neck with boiling water. Seal with lid and ring, and leave for 3 months, or all winter.

This is my sister-in-law Lete's way of putting up sauerkraut, and you don't have the strong odor that comes from fermenting it in a crock.

TOMATO JUICE

2½ pounds ripe tomatoes
1½ cups water
½ cup watercress, washed and stemmed
3 stalks celery, chopped
1 medium onion, sliced
½ medium green pepper, cut in strips
1 teaspoon salt

Wash tomatoes, remove cores and cut in quarters. Put in a pan with ½ cup water and simmer until soft. Rub through a strainer or food mill.

Put the juice in a pan with the remaining 1 cup water, watercress, celery, onion, green pepper, and salt. Bring to a boil, reduce heat, and simmer 20 minutes, until vegetables are soft. Strain the liquid and either bottle and refrigerate or pour into hot sterilized jars and seal. Makes 1 quart.

MINCEMEAT

We always made plenty of mincemeat because we ate mince pies all year, hot in winter and cold in summer, and in any case, it is so much work that there's not much point in making a small amount. You can keep mincemeat for a long time when it is sealed in jars, and of course, homemade mincemeat makes a very welcome Christmas gift. I've also found that mincemeat pie, like shoofly pie, freezes well.

      5 pounds hamburger
      2 quarts dried apples, soaked
      5 pounds cooking apples, cored and peeled
      4 lemons
      1 pound raisins
      1 pound currants
    1½ pounds brown sugar
      1 quart table molasses
      1 cup cider vinegar
      3 cups strong-flavored wine
      1 teaspoon cinnamon
      1 teaspoon nutmeg
      1 teaspoon ground cloves

Cook the hamburger over medium heat in a heavy skillet, breaking it up with a wooden spoon, until all traces of pink have disappeared. The meat should be cooked through, but not browned.

Put the soaked dried apples through a meat grinder. Grind the cooking apples coarsely. Grind the lemons, peel and all. (If you don't have a meat grinder, these can be done in a blender.)

Combine the hamburger, ground fruit, and all the remaining ingredients in a heavy pot, bring to a boil, reduce the heat, and simmer for 30 minutes, stirring to combine well. Ladle into sterilized quart jars and seal. Makes about 8 quarts.

APPLE BUTTER

When we made apple butter at home, we cooked it in a big copper kettle on the Farmer's Friend, an old-fashioned wood-burning stove that stood about twenty inches from the floor. It had graduated plates on the top, from the largest, big enough to take the copper kettle, on down to a center one just the right size for a tea kettle. The Farmer's Friend was usually right outside the kitchen, next to the coal bin, and that was where you made your apple butter, blanched corn, cooked pork pudding, and did all your quantity cooking, keeping the steam and the heat out of the kitchen. It was strictly for top-of-the-stove cooking.

The fire for the apple butter was started early in the morning; and there'd be eight hours of everyone taking his turn stirring with the big heart-shaped wooden paddle that had a hole in the middle so the apple butter went through the center, too, and didn't stick. It was a real family get-together; everyone visited and ate, and took home their crocks full of apple butter. I'm glad I could see and do all that when I was young; it was a lot of fun.

I remember that the day before the apple butter boiling we'd go for the apples for cider and snitz and get as many as twenty 100-pound sacks—and that's a lot of apples. We had one of those funny old-fashioned apple peelers and we kids —there'd be maybe two or three of us—would see how fast we could crank it. There was always an apple on the peeler. As it kicked one off, you'd have the next one ready to go; it was fun seeing just how fast you could do it. You made a game of it, getting a kick from competing against your-self. Then when you'd finished, you could go swimming; that spurred you on to get the job done quickly. Recently I found one of the old apple peelers, and my kids are just as ex-cited about that thing as I was.

> 12 pounds tart cooking apples, peeled, cored, and quartered
>   (in the fall, use winesap apples)
> 2 cups water

3½ cups granulated sugar
1 cup cider vinegar
1 teaspoon cinnamon

Cook the apples and water in a pan over low heat until soft, about 20 minutes. Rub through a food mill.

Add the sugar, cider vinegar, and cinnamon, mixing well. Put mixture in a heavy roaster pan, uncovered, and cook in a 375° oven for approximately 2½ hours, stirring every 15 minutes with a wooden spoon. The apple butter is thick enough when you can put 2 tablespoons of the mixture on a saucer and turn it upside down without its dropping off.

Ladle into hot sterilized pint or quart jars and seal. Makes about 3½ quarts, or 7 pints.

AUNT MIRIAM'S RASPBERRY JELLY

There's a goodness and fresh flavor about homemade jellies that you never get with the commercial kind. I've yet to find anyone who isn't delighted and touched to be given a little pot of your homemade jelly. I look out for small pretty containers to use instead of jars; if sealed with a layer of paraffin, the jelly keeps well.

One quart raspberries or other juicy berries usually yields 2 cups juice. Cover the raspberries with water, bring to a boil, reduce heat and cook slowly, uncovered, until fruit is soft and juice flows freely. Pour into a jelly bag that has been wrung out in water and suspended over a bowl. Allow the juice to drip through. Do not squeeze the bag or juice will be cloudy.

Take the 2 cups raspberry juice (or juice from other berries, such as wineberries, blackberries, blueberries) and combine in a 6- to 8-quart preserving kettle with 2 cups sugar, 2 tablespoons cider vinegar, and ½ teaspoon cream of tartar. Bring to a boil, and boil until jelly reaches a temperature of 225°.

Cool for 10 minutes and skim off the froth. Cool for another 10 minutes before ladling into sterilized ½-pint jars or jelly glasses. Seal jars with lids and rings. Makes 1½ pints.

Note: If you use jelly glasses that don't have self-sealing vacuum-type lids, fill to within ¼ inch of the top and then pour on a thin layer of melted paraffin, making sure it covers the jelly completely and reaches to all sides of the glass. If any air bubbles appear, prick them with a knife. Leave the glasses until the paraffin is cold and hard, then cover with the lid.

STRAWBERRY PRESERVES

1½ pounds sugar
1 cup water
1 quart strawberries

Combine the sugar and water in a pan, bring to a boil, and boil briskly about 2 minutes. Add the washed and hulled strawberries. Boil, skimming occasionally and stirring with a wooden spoon to prevent sticking, until mixture reaches a temperature of 225°. Check to see if it will jell by putting a little of the preserves on an ice-cold saucer. If not, boil until it will set when tested. Ladle into sterilized jars or jelly glasses and seal. Makes 1½ pints.

PINEAPPLE PRESERVES

   1 quart crushed canned pineapple
   1 cup water (scant)
2½ pounds sugar
     Juice of ½ large lemon

Combine the ingredients in a preserving kettle and bring to a boil. Boil, stirring occasionally to prevent sticking, until mixture reaches a temperature of 230°. Test for setting, as above. Ladle into jars or jelly glasses and seal. Makes 3 pints.

This is a very old and rare gallon jar used for canning meats.

CHAPTER VI

Wine Makes the Heart Merry

WINEMAKING is an engrossing hobby, and one in which you never reach perfection. It's relaxing, because this is such a natural and elemental process; challenging, because there is always more to learn, and very rewarding. What better gift can you give a friend than the fruits of your labors?

As I mentioned before, I got into winemaking by accident. When I was a child, I wasn't even aware that the farm people in our neighborhood made wine. Although it was used

228

in mincemeat and as a folk medicine—dandelion wine for a spring tonic, elderberry wine for a cold—I can't remember ever having seen it made. Winemaking has only come out in the open in the last forty years, mainly because our church changed its attitude towards wine. The Amish, who are very strict about their religion, are the first to admit that they always made wine.

After all, as I said to Daddy one time when he was being a little bit disapproving about my winemaking activities, it does say in Psalms, "He maketh the grass to grow for the cattle, and wine to make man's heart merry." "All right," Daddy said. "That only mentions men. Where does it say anything about women?" That didn't stop me for one minute. "Now you know very well," I told him, "that as long as the men are happy, the women will be too."

When I got married and needed wine for mincemeat, I took the advice of my neighbors and made my own from the juice of canned fruits. I wasn't too sure how my husband would feel about my making wine; so I didn't ask his permission. That's probably the only secret I have ever kept from him.

One morning Mother came to see me, and I poured some of my wine into a big water goblet and asked her what she thought of it. I'll always remember her answer. "It's very pretty, but don't acquire a taste for it." That has become a standard saying in our family ever since: "Don't acquire a taste for it."

I put the glass on the kitchen counter and when Abe came in for his noontime meal I mustered all my nerve and said, "I have a surprise for you. How would you like to taste my wine?"

I went over to the counter and found the glass empty. I couldn't think what had happened, until suddenly I heard someone singing upstairs. It was an Amish girl who came to clean for me one day a week. There she was with the sweeper running, singing her head off—and usually the Amish don't sing very loud. I called to her and she came flying down the back stairs. When I asked if she'd seen anything on the counter she answered, "Ach yes, I did. I looked at it and thought it was wine; then I tasted it and it *was* wine and do you know, it was good? You don't mind I drank it all?" No wonder she was singing!

Every year I'd make 3 gallons of wine and use 2 or 2½ gallons for mincemeat, leaving the rest on the cellar shelf. After Erma goofed and put it in the Harvard beets, thinking it was vinegar, and they made such a hit with the guests, I decided I'd better go in for winemaking in earnest.

I really didn't know much about it, and there were no grapes available; so the first thing I thought of was dandelion wine, because we always have millions of dandelions in the meadows and it's very traditional in our area. My doctor was on a winemaking binge just then, and he gave me some of his recipes. The first batch I made came out perfectly and after that I was hooked. The more wines I made, the more I enjoyed finding out how different the results were from the various fruits and flowers and vegetables. You have to persevere when you make wine and I'm an impatient person to a degree. I knew I lacked patience and I made wine to acquire it. Now I've gained patience and lost my humility.

As I learned how to make my wines dryer, Abe, who doesn't care for sweet wines, got to like them, and to participate. Of course it is the man, as head of the household, who applies for the permit to make the 200 gallons a year you are allowed for family use. He would do a lot of the heavy work. I'd start the wine; then he would taste it after it had fermented and tell me when he thought it was right, putting his stamp of approval on it.

Once you get started making wine, there's no hope for

The longer you make wine, the more you learn.

you. You find you have to keep going and learning. Wine-making has become a family hobby; we are all into it. We go out together to pick berries. The children crush the fruit and stomp the grapes. Abe has started a vineyard of hybrid grapes, and we're anxious to see which do best and produce well in our soil.

Pennsylvania is a good growing area. It was here that William Penn developed the Concord from the native wild fox grape, and everyone around our part of the country makes Concord wine, mostly sweet. I've discovered that if you want to make a dry wine from Concord grapes, the secret is to pick the grapes early, before they are fully ripe, while they are still slightly green on the top. Then you get a beautiful light dry wine with almost no trace of the foxy Concord flavor. As the grapes are underripe you have to add sugar to help it along, but within a year and a half or two years you'll have a delightful wine.

I also discovered that certain fruit wines—apricot and the dry Concord particularly—are enhanced by a wood flavor; so I make them in glass and age them in a 10-gallon, charred-oak keg, which clears the wine and gives it the oak flavor. You can buy charred-oak barrels from whiskey companies for about $15.

As we don't have a wine license, we don't serve or sell wine in the restaurant, but after dinner we invite the guests to go down and see the wine cellar and have a tiny complimentary taste—and do they love it. One evening there was this very sober and serious lady who hadn't said a word all night, nothing seemed to loosen her up. I was describing the wines and I said, "This one is rather unusual; we call it the pucker-power wine because it's made from wild persimmons." She elected to have that, so I gave her a taste and all of a sudden everything got kind of quiet and she looked up and said, "Do you have a small straw?" There she was all puckered up from the tart persimmons.

To tell you everything you should know about home winemaking would fill a book, and there are some excellent ones on the subject that I'll mention later. To start you off, here is Betty's Capsule Course in Winemaking.

WHAT YOU NEED TO MAKE WINE AT HOME

For crushing the fruit and the primary fermentation, you need heavy, lidded 1½-gallon plastic pails that can be sterilized (never use copper, aluminum, iron, or galvanized pails or tubs). If you are making a large quantity of grape wine, it is best to use a charred-oak whiskey barrel with one end open. The crushed grapes are put in the open barrel and stirred daily for 10 days before being pressed. Then the juice is put in kegs or glass for the secondary fermentation. To crush small amounts of fruit, a wooden potato masher works pretty well.

For the secondary fermentation, use large glass jugs or carboys with a capacity of 1 to 5 gallons (larger sizes are hard to handle when full). Save the gallon and half-gallon wine jugs you get from your liquor store. These can be used to ferment small batches of wine.

To seal the jugs or carboys, you need a fermentation lock, a piece of glass tubing bent into a U-shaped loop, with two round bubbles in the upright parts of the U. This fits into a drilled cork or stopper in the neck of the jug. The fermentation lock is partly filled with water to keep out the air and bacteria. The escaping carbon dioxide gas formed during fermentation forces its way through the water seal, forming little bubbles. When no more bubbles appear, the wine has stopped fermenting and can be siphoned into a clean glass jug. This process, known as racking, clears the wine and removes it from the sediment at the bottom of the fermenting jug.

The siphon, a length of plastic tubing about 6 to 8 feet long and $\frac{1}{4}$ inch in diameter, can be bought with a suction wine pump; but I prefer the old way of sucking on one end of the hose until the wine flows through.

The two essential testing instruments for the winemaker are a hydrometer and a vinometer. The hydrometer enables

A cluster of wines fermenting in the cellar.

you to gauge the amount of natural sugar in the juice, so you know how much more to add, and to check on the fermenting process. The vinometer measures the alcohol content of the finished wine.

To store and age the finished wine, you will need plenty of bottles. You can buy new wine bottles in the traditional shapes and colors, but if you are a wine drinker, it is easier to save your old wine bottles, washing them in hot water with a detergent, rinsing and drying thoroughly. A dishwasher, which has a much higher water temperature than your hands can stand, is good for washing the bottles, and you can sterilize them completely by putting them in a 275° oven for 15 minutes (make sure they are hot when they go in; otherwise they may crack).

A hand corker is a must if you are going to cork rather than cap your wine bottles. I much prefer to cork and seal bottles. They can then be laid on their sides in the wine rack without any fear of leaking or rusting. Capping is all right if you intend to drink the wine quickly, but I like to cork and age my wines. Corks should be sterilized in boiling water before being inserted.

Labels are, of course, essential to identify the type of wine and the date it was made and bottled. You can use ordinary gummed labels, but it is more fun to have one that is original and personal. Winemaker's shops sell these, as well as other basic equipment; or, if you are artistically inclined, you can design your own and have it reproduced.

Winemaker's shops, which I find more fascinating to shop in than boutiques, will also supply you with Campden tablets and wine yeast, which you need when fermenting wine. Campden tablets are a pressed form of potassium metabisulfite, a fungicide that suppresses the bacteria, molds, and wild yeasts that can attack and destroy wine in its early stages, when the fruit is freshly crushed. The wine yeast, added with sugar syrup to the crushed fruit, starts the primary fermentation.

There's always enough wine on hand to give each of the guests a little taste after dinner.

METHODS OF MAKING WINE

Most wine recipes follow much the same rule of thumb. Allow 3-4 pounds of fruit for 1 gallon wine, 1½-2 pounds sugar per gallon for dry wine, 2½ pounds per gallon for a sweet wine. If the fruit you are using is very sweet, like apples, you will need less sugar.

To make many wines, the sugar is boiled with water to a syrup, cooled, and then added in three parts. The yeast ferments better if the sugar is introduced in stages, rather than all at one time.

*I age some of the sweeter, heavier wines rather longer,
as you can see by the dust on the bottles.*

The two methods of winemaking I'm going to give you, which are those I follow, are adapted from *Successful Wine Making at Home* by H. E. Bravery, a small paperback published by Arco Books. One of my guests sent it to me years ago and I have found it invaluable. Other good books for the home winemaker are *Folk Wines, Cordials and Brandies* by M. A. Jagendorf, published by Vanguard Press, *American Wines and Winemaking* by Philip Wagner (available from Boordy Vineyards, Box 38, Riderwood, Md. 21139), and *Home Winemaker's Handbook* by Walter S. Taylor and Richard P. Vine, published by Harper & Row. The two latter books are exclusively about making wine from grapes and really authoritative.

Walter Taylor is the owner of Bully Hill Vineyards, from whose nursery we bought our hybrid grape cuttings, and Richard Vine was the winemaker for the Pleasant Valley Wine Company.

WINEMAKING METHOD NO. 1
(FERMENTED PULP)

Crush fruit by hand in a plastic pail. Add 1 quart boiled and cooled water and mix well. Dissolve 1 crushed Campden tablet in ¼ cup warm water and mix with the pulp. Leave for 1 or 2 hours.

Meanwhile, make a syrup of the sugar and water in the proportions given in each recipe, boiling the dissolved sugar and water for 1 minute. Cool the syrup and divide into three parts.

Stir 1 part of the cooled syrup into the pulp. Add 1 teaspoon wine yeast and cover the pail, either with the lid or with a sheet of plastic secured with string. As the plastic is porous, the gas from this primary fermentation will find a way out, but no airborne bacteria will find a way in. Allow to ferment for 1 week.

Strain the pulp through cheesecloth and wring out as dry as possible. Discard the pulp and put the strained juice into a clean gallon jug. Add the second part of the syrup. Fit fermentation lock into the neck of the jug and ferment in a warm place (65° to 70°) for 10 days.

Siphon the wine into another clean gallon jug, leaving as much of the sediment behind as possible. Add the remaining third part of the syrup, put the fermentation lock back in the neck of the jug and leave it in a warm place until all fermentation ceases.

Note: I like to taste the wine before adding the third part of the syrup to see whether or not it needs more.

WINEMAKING METHOD NO. 2
(FERMENTED JUICE)

Crush the fruit by hand, as before, add the 1 quart boiled, cooled water, mix well, and add the Campden tablet. Leave in a cool place for 24 hours, stirring twice during that time. Strain through cheesecloth and squeeze gently, not too hard as you only want the juice. Discard the pulp.

Make the sugar syrup as before, and cool. Add ⅓ of the syrup and 1 teaspoon wine yeast, cover, and ferment for 10 days.

Siphon the wine into a clean gallon jug, leaving behind as much deposit as possible. Add second third of syrup, plug neck of jug with fermentation lock, and ferment in a warm place for 2 weeks.

At this point, taste the wine, and, according to whether you like your wine sweet or dry, add the final third of syrup, if necessary. Refit the fermentation lock and leave until all fermentation ceases.

WINES MADE BY METHOD NO. 1

STRAWBERRY WINE

    4 pounds fresh strawberries
2½ pounds sugar (for a very dry wine, 2 pounds)
    4 quarts water

Crush the fruit, make a syrup of the sugar and water, and follow method No. 1. Makes 1 gallon.

WINEBERRY WINE

3½ pounds wineberries (wild red raspberries)
2½ pounds sugar
  4 quarts water

Crush the fruit, make a syrup of the sugar and water, and follow method No. 1. Makes 1 gallon.

CRANBERRY WINE

3 quarts cranberries, chopped
4 quarts boiling water
3 pounds sugar

Put the cranberries in a pail and pour the boiling water over them. Follow Method No. 1, adding the sugar in three stages. Makes 1 gallon.

Note: This makes a flavorful, tart wine, good to use in cooking.

1

APRICOT WINE

    4 pounds fresh apricots
1½ to 2 pounds sugar, depending on the sweetness of the fruit
    4 quarts water

Crush the fruit. Make a syrup with the sugar and water and follow Method No. 1. Makes 1 gallon.

CONCORD GRAPE WINE

    8 pounds Concord grapes
1¼ pounds sugar
    2 quarts water

Stem the grapes before crushing them. Make a syrup with the sugar and water and follow Method No. 1. Makes 1 gallon.

3

1. Johnny and friend Barb Miller have fun stomping the grapes for wine. 2. Feet get washed before and after stomping. 3. Ron Lutz and the Stahl boys tip the stomped grapes into pans and tubs. 4. Everyone sits down and takes a hand stemming the crushed grapes.

4

END-OF-THE-DAY WINE

This is our name for the wine from all the fresh or canned fruits that aren't going to make it to the next day. Rather than throw them out, I put them in a pail and let them ferment, now and then sprinkling on some sugar to help the fermentation along. You can use berries, apricots, lemons, oranges—even banana peels. If you peel your peaches too thick, add the parings, and some of the peach pits, which help to clarify the wine.

> 2 quarts of any fresh or canned fruit
> 1 pound sugar
> 3 quarts water

Crush the fruit. Make a syrup with the sugar and water. Follow Method No. 1. Makes 1 gallon.

Note: If only fruit juices are used, follow Method No. 2, fermenting 3 quarts strained juice.

WINE MADE BY METHOD NO. 2

––––––––––

Remember *Arsenic and Old Lace,* and the little old ladies who liquidated visitors with their elderberry wine? This is the only berry wine, it seems, that masks the taste of arsenic. Apart from that, it tastes great, especially when it is on the verge of being too dry.

ELDERBERRY WINE

3½ pounds elderberries
2½ pounds sugar
4 quarts water

Crush the fruit. Make a syrup with the sugar and water. Follow Method No. 2, fermenting the strained juice. Makes 1 gallon.

WINES MADE FROM FLOWERS

As flowers have no natural sugar, these wines are made differently from the fruit wines.

RED CLOVER BLOSSOM WINE

3 quarts clover heads (without stalks)
3 quarts boiling water
2 lemons, sliced
1½ pounds sugar
2 cups water
1 teaspoon wine yeast

Pour the boiling water over the clover and let stand overnight. Next day, strain liquid and add lemons. Make a syrup of the sugar and water. Cool syrup. Add to the liquid with the wine yeast. Ferment in a covered container for seven days, stirring each day. Strain the liquid.

Make a syrup with 1 pound sugar and 2 cups water. Cool the syrup, add to the strained liquid, and pour into a gallon jug. Fit with a fermentation lock and leave in a warm place until all fermentation has ceased. Makes 1 gallon.

DANDELION WINE

 3 quarts dandelion heads (without stalks)
 3 quarts boiling water
 3 oranges, sliced
 3 lemons, sliced
 1 pound seedless raisins
1½ pounds sugar
 1 quart water
 1 teaspoon wine yeast

Pour the boiling water over the dandelion heads and let stand, covered, overnight. Next day, strain through cheesecloth, pressing until dry.

Put strained liquid in a plastic pail and add oranges, lemons, raisins, and sugar syrup made from the sugar and 1 quart water. Add the wine yeast. Cover and ferment for 15 days, stirring every day.

Strain fermented juice through cheesecloth and add a cooled syrup made from 1 pound sugar and 2 cups water.

Pour into a gallon jug, fit with a fermentation lock and leave in a warm place until all fermentation has ceased. Makes 1 gallon.

LOCUST BLOSSOM WINE

 3 quarts locust blossoms (without stalks)
 3 quarts boiling water
 1 orange, sliced
 1 lemon, sliced
 2 to 2½ pounds sugar
 1 quart water
 1 well-beaten egg white
 1 teaspoon wine yeast

Pour the boiling water over the locust blossoms and let stand overnight. Next day, strain the liquid and add the orange and

Dandelion Wine

1 qt. dandelion flowers scald with 1 qt
boiling water let stand 24 hrs. then press
1 cup yeast 1 lemon 4 lbs sugar.

lemon. Make a syrup of the sugar and water, boiling for 1 minute. Cool. Add ⅓ of cooled syrup to liquid. Fold in beaten egg white (this clarifies the wine) and yeast. Ferment in a covered container for seven days. Strain through cheesecloth. Put the strained juice into a gallon jug, add a second ⅓ of syrup, and fit fermentation lock into neck of jug. Ferment in a warm place for 10 days. Siphon into a clean gallon jug, taste the wine and, if necessary, add the remaining syrup, according to how sweet you like your wine. This is a honey-sweet dessert wine, with a beautiful golden color and a headily perfumed bouquet from the fragrant locust blossoms, delicious to sip with a creamy dessert, or in a fruit compote.

OTHER WINES

APPLE WINE

  3 quarts fresh unpasteurized apple cider
½ pound sugar
½ pound raisins
  1 teaspoon wine yeast

Freshly pressed cider, which you can buy in apple country in the fall, is a different thing from the sweet cider sold in supermarkets, in which the natural fermentation has been stopped by pasteurization, or the addition of preservatives.

    Combine the apple cider, sugar, raisins, and yeast in a

fermenting pail or crock. Cover and let stand for 15 days, stirring every other day.

Strain the fermented juice and pour into a gallon jug. Fit with fermentation lock and leave in a warm place until all fermentation has ceased. Makes 1 gallon.

Fruit and flower wines are good to cook with as well as to drink, but wines made from root vegetables such as beets and potatoes are not. Although they are pleasant to sip, the flavor is too bland for cooking and they have no bouquet.

Beet wine is one of the oldest folk wines. I read somewhere that when Hannibal crossed the Alps he fortified his men with beet wine, and fed them raisins for energy. I told this story one night in the wine cellar and one man asked why beet wine. I said, "That's how they got the elephants so high. What do you think?"

BEET WINE

    5 to 6 beets, about the size of a tea cup
    3 pounds sugar
    3 dashes pepper
    1 slice toast
    1 teaspoon wine yeast

Cook the beets in water to cover until tender. Remove beets. (They can be used for pickled beets.) Measure beet liquid and add enough water to make 1 gallon. Add sugar and pepper, bring to a boil, and boil 10 minutes.

Strain the liquid and cool. When cool, put in a crock or vat and float the toast on top, with yeast on the toast. (This is called top fermentation, which means the wine ferments from the top).

Cover and ferment for seven days. Strain and pour into a gallon jug fitted with a fermentation lock. Leave in a warm place until all fermentation has ceased. Makes 1 gallon.

EQUIPMENT SUPPLIERS FOR HOME WINEMAKERS

Milan Laboratories
57 Spring Street
New York, N.Y. 10012

The Winemaker's Shop
Bully Hill Road
Hammondsport, N.Y. 14840
   (*Home Winemaker's Handbook* is available from The Winemaker's Shop.)

The Compleat Winemaker
P.O. Box 2470
Yountville, Ca. 94599

Presque Isle Wine Cellars
9440 Buffalo Road
North East, Pa. 16428

F. H. Steinbart Company
526 S.E. Grand Avenue
Portland, Oreg. 97214

Vino Corporation
Box 7885
Rochester, N.Y. 14606

Aetna Wine Supplies
708 Rainier Avenue South
Seattle, Wash. 98144

Jim's Home Beverage Supplies
North 2613 Division Street
Spokane, Wash. 99207

Boordy Vineyards
Riderwood, Md. 21139
   (Nursery grape stock. Philip Wagner's two books, *A Wine Grower's Guide* and *American Wines and Wine Making*, may be ordered from the above address for $6.95 each, plus $.35 postage and handling charge.)

Index

249